D0392628

YOU'RE SAYING IT WRONG

YOU'RE SAYING IT WRONG

A PRONUNCIATION GUIDE TO
THE 150 MOST COMMONLY
MISPRONOUNCED WORDS AND THEIR
TANGLED HISTORIES OF MISUSE

ROSS PETRAS AND KATHRYN PETRAS

TEN SPEED PRESS
Berkeley

CONTENTS

ACKNOWLEDGMENTS

Thanks to our ever-fantastic agent Andrea Somberg and our wonderfully "persnickety dastardly editor" Lisa Westmoreland, as well as our expert copy editor Elisabeth Beller, senior designer Chloe Rawlins, and the rest of the team at Ten Speed. And a special thanks to our families— Sylvia and Alex, and Randy, Micheal, and Yvonne—for putting up with us correcting their (and our own) pronunciation.

INTRODUCTION

We've all been there. You're at a party, talking to someone you want to impress, trying to sound superintellectual, when wham! You toss in some ostensibly impressive word or term and then realize by the expression on your listener's face that you completely blew it by mispronouncing said word or term.

It's indeed a common problem and a common worry. A 2015 study conducted for Dictionary.com found that 47 percent of all Americans are irritated by mispronunciations and correct their family and friends. Millennials—aged eighteen to thirty-four—are the pickiest: 63 percent of them confess to correcting other people's mistakes. Across the pond in Great Britain, where English began, it's a similar situation. A recent study commissioned by St. Pancras International found that nearly a quarter of all British people are so worried about getting certain words wrong that they actually ask someone else to say them. One in six say they stop the conversation to apologize for their mispronunciation. But a whopping 41 percent go on the attack and stop a conversation to correct someone else. Thus this book.

We call these mispronounced words "shibboleth words." These are the words that can trip you up, mix you up, and make you sound like an ignoramus . . . right when you're trying to sound intellectual (or at least not like an ignoramus!).

But why the term *shibboleth words*? What is a shibboleth? Technically, a shibboleth is a custom or mode of speaking, behaving, or believing that distinguishes one group of people from another. The word *shibboleth* itself comes from the Hebrew word *shibbóleth* (שִׁיבֹּלֶת), which literally means "grain stalks." What do grain stalks have to do with pronunciation? Quite a bit, if you were an ancient Ephraimite. In biblical times, during a war with the Ephraimites, the equally ancient Gileadites used to ask people crossing the boundary River Jordan to say the word. The Gileadites could say the shibboleth "correctly," but the enemy Ephraimites couldn't pronounce the *sh*—and so, by the sound of a pair of letters, they were identified as the enemy and killed. Even more recently, British commandos in World War II used an identification-code shibboleth—*squirrel*—since the Germans usually pronounced it "skwiv-er-el"; mispronouncers faced the same dire penalty as the ancient *sh*-less Ephraimites. Fortunately, the penalties aren't so severe nowadays. Humiliation beats death. But it's still mortifying, if not mortal.

This is the prime reason for this book: to help us all avoid that unpleasant mortification that ensues when we attempt to use one of the surprisingly large number of words that we have absolutely no idea how to say properly. *You're Saying It Wrong* not only tells you how to correctly pronounce these shibboleth words, but also discusses their origins, delves into some fascinating word facts and histories, and examines why so many of us don't know how to pronounce these words correctly. The specific words and phrases we've chosen are the ones that smart people most commonly mispronounce, the ones that appear on lists and in dictionary surveys, and those we ourselves found the most confounding.

One important note: While some of these shibboleth words do have a correct pronunciation and an incorrect one, according to the dictionary, others are more fluid. In some cases, so many people mispronounce a word that the new (originally wrong) pronunciation slowly becomes accepted . . . and sometimes even preferred. (Chalk up another point for English as a growing language.) In other cases, there are two or more acceptable pronunciations. And in still others, certain groups or regions have one pronunciation, while others have their own. We've tried to be clear in covering these different instances.

We also must mention that when it comes to pronunciation inclusion, some dictionaries are very, shall we say, exuberant? Maybe a little too exuberant (we're not naming names). Their motto seems to be, "We include every pronunciation we've ever heard of this word!" In this book, we've tried to keep it a little more streamlined and present the preferred pronunciations, not the whole shebang (pronounced "shuh-BANG," by the way), the ones most dictionaries, linguists, and generally knowledgeable Americans agree upon.

That brings us to another point: some people argue that, since languages change, we should just "get used to it," that there's no such thing as "preferred" or "correct" pronunciation at all. Yes, English keeps changing, but we must add that most linguistic changes (consonantal drift and the like) take at least decades. (If you chatted about "horshwoel" now, no one would know what you were talking about. But that's how you used to say *walrus*.)

So we're in the camp of the "Why not pronounce it the way most people say it should be pronounced now?" school. We also have made American pronunciation the default. British English has its own sound. We reached our conclusions by drawing on such definitive tomes as the *Oxford English Dictionary*, the *American Heritage Dictionary*, the *Cambridge English Dictionary*, *Merriam-Webster's Collegiate Dictionary*, and *Webster's Third New International Dictionary*, and by reading linguistics blogs, journals, articles, and surveys on pronunciation and, even more helpfully, mispronunciation.

All that said, we hope you find the book as enlightening as we found it while collecting these shibboleth words. (Confession: In the process of doing this book, we discovered quite a few words we'd been mispronouncing all along. Live and learn!)

TWO IMPORTANT NOTES TO KEEP IN MIND WHEN READING THIS BOOK

First, although we said it earlier, it bears repeating: Some dictionaries include virtually all pronunciations of a word, including those that are slangy or generally regarded as incorrect. We do not; we include only those that are generally regarded as correct or preferred. Second: we've indicated how to pronounce words a bit unscientifically, according to what looks easiest and most accurate for a given word. Sometimes one way of writing a sound looked easier to understand than another way, and so we erred on the side of ease of comprehension rather than consistency. Also, although many dictionaries use special symbols such as the famous (or infamous) schwa sound symbol (ə) we've avoided such symbols when showing how a word should sound. We use CAPITAL letters to indicate where the stress should be. And that's about it. Enjoy—or rather, en-JOI!

acai

[ah-sigh-EE]

*species of palm tree from the Amazon rain forest,
best known for its health-giving reddish-purple berry*

It is difficult not to run across acai berries nowadays. They're called a superfood and frequently turn up in juice blends and supplements. So it's a pity that so many of us can't say the word correctly. On a Starbucks blog, one employee confidently said it's pronounced "ak-a-ee," while another called him an idiot. That's a bit too much acrimony over a tart berry, so let's play peacemaker: It's not ACK-ah-ee, it's not ah-KAI, and it's not ah-SIGH. It's ah-sigh-EE, with a soft *c* and a stress on the last syllable.

For the spelling that tricks many English speakers, you can blame the early Portuguese explorers of Brazil, who saw indigenous rain-forest people eating a strange and luscious palm tree berry that they called in their Tupi-Guarani language *ïwaca'i* (something that cries or expels water). The Portuguese wrote this down as *açaí*, but in Portuguese the *c* comes with a squiggly cedilla at the bottom that makes the *c* sound soft, and there's an accent on the *i*. The result is something very close to the original pronunciation. Since English doesn't come equipped with softening cedillas and accents, the result is a very untasteful rendering of a very tasty fruit.

aegis

[EE-gis] (also [AY-gis])

the protection and/or support of a powerful,
knowledgeable, or benevolent person or organization

To paraphrase the old song, "You say 'AY-gis,' I say 'EE-gis'/
Let's call the whole thing off."

Yes, let's. The so-called proper pronunciation of *aegis*
in American English has long been "EE-gis," with a long *e*
sound, even though the classical Latin it came from would
have the *ae* as an "eye" or an "a-ee." But more recently,
dictionaries like *Merriam Webster* have allowed a second
pronunciation in—"AY-gis" . . . possibly because so many
people were already saying it that way.

We use it now most typically in a phrase like "under the
aegis of" to signify being under someone or something's
protection, but in ancient times, it meant "under the
protection of a goatskin shield," something not particularly
useful today. *Aegis* is a Latin word that comes from the
ancient Greek *aigis*—which, as used in the *Iliad*, refers to
something goat-based, for lack of a better term (*aigos* [goat]),
carried by Zeus and Athena for protection. Zeus's *aigis* was
a goatskin shield; Athena's was an *aigis* 2.0—a goatskin cloak
covered in scales, bordered with snakes, and containing a
gorgon's head.

aerie (also eyrie)

[AIR-ee, EER-ee]

nest of an eagle or other bird of prey, often referring to nests on mountaintops or cliffs

What's a modern eagle lover to do? Say "AIR-ee," "EER-ee," or "EYE-ree"? Short of just calling it "an eagle's nest," we can go to the dictionaries.

There have been a variety of spellings and pronunciations from the beginning. *Aerie* probably comes from the Latin *ager* (field or place in the sense of an eagle's place). This became the late Latin *aerius* (nest), and then, by way of the Norman conquerors of England, *air* from the Middle French *aire*. (The "air" in *debonair* comes from the same root meaning.) It was sometimes called an *ere* or *eire*—which probably spawned the alternate spelling and pronunciation.

Here in America, *Merriam Webster's* prefers the spelling *aerie*, pronounced "AIR-ee." The *Cambridge Dictionary* likes *eyrie* ("EER-ee"). The venerable *Oxford English Dictionary* covers all the bases, preferring *eyrie* and "EER-ee" but also listing *aerie*, noting that Americans usually pronounce both spellings as "AIR-ee." It also notes in its characteristic understated way, "The pronunciation history of the word presents a number of points of difficulty, which have not been adequately explained" and suggests that we might wish to consult *Französisches etymol. Wörterbuch XXV. 1318/1–1325/1*. We suggest you just toss a coin.

albeit

[all-BEE-it]

although, despite

It's never properly pronounced "all-BITE" or "ALL-bite," although that's what many people say. The problem is that we usually first encounter *albeit* in print: because the *beit* part of the word looks a bit like German, "bite" sounds like a reasonable way to end this odd-looking word.

Technically, *albeit* is a contraction from the Middle English of what was originally a three-word phrase "al[though] it [may] be." It had a past tense ("all were it") that no one uses today. *Albeit* also had a poor cousin, now virtually unknown: *howbeit*, meaning "nevertheless" and "how[ever] it [may] be." Howbeit, don't worry about all the grammar and history, and remember how to pronounce *albeit* . . . or just say "although" instead. How about that?

alumnae

[uh-LUM-nee]

female graduates or former students

Here's a very quick Latin lesson for alumni of any schools, colleges, or universities. *Alumnus* is a male former student or graduate, *alumna* is a female, *alumni* is the plural of males and of male and female graduates together. *Alumnae* is the plural for only female graduates, since *ae* is a feminine ending.

And now for the annoying part, at least for students of Latin: English took some Latin endings and changed their pronunciation. Latin students pronounce the *ae* as "eye" and the *i* as "ee" while in English, it's the opposite. What to do? One of us who reads Latin winces but still we both think that when in England (or the United States, Canada, etc.) do as the English speakers do. So in English, *alumnae* is pronounced "uh-LUM-nee," and *alumni* is pronounced "uh-LUM-nigh." And that's how you should pronounce them. After all, you're graduating from a university or other school, not a *universitatis* or *schola*.

Antarctica

[ant-ARK-tik-a]

relating to the regions, flora, and fauna around the South Pole

Mispronouncing this word as "an-ART-ik-a" is usually a matter of laziness rather than lack of knowledge. Most of us are aware of the *t* sound following the *n*, and the *k* sound following the *r*, but if we're talking quickly we omit one or both.

Although *Antarctic* came from the Latin word *antarcticus*, by the Latin Dark Ages and the Medieval French era, the hard *c* or *k* sound was lost. The earliest known use of the word in the polar sense is from 1270, *Cercle antartike*, with no *k* after the *r*, and there are other medieval references to *antartique*, again without the *k* sound after the *r*. Learned (or maybe just snobby) Renaissance scholars later put it back to conform to the more prestigious Latin, and today, we're back to pronouncing it more as the ancients would have.

The word *arctic* refers to bears and came to refer to the North Pole regions due to the constellation containing the North Star—Ursa Major, the Great Bear. (*Ursa* is "female bear" in Latin; *arktos* is "bear" in ancient Greek; *artikos* means "pertaining to a bear.") And so Antarctica is a combined word—*anti* (opposite) the *arktos* (bear), or "opposite the Arctic."

antipodes

[an-TIP-uh-deez]

geographic term meaning situated on the opposite side of the globe; places on earth directly opposite each other; also generally opposite

First a look at the origins of this strange word: It comes from ancient Greek—*anti* (opposite) and *podes* (the Greek plural for *pous* [foot])—in other words, "opposite the feet." So people who have the soles of their feet over (or under) where we have the soles of our feet are on the other side of the world.

It looks like it should be pronounced "an-TEE-podes" (to rhyme with *toads*), but it most certainly isn't. When a word that starts with "anti-" has been imported into English from the ancient Greek or Latin and is followed by two syllables, the accent usually falls on the second syllable— as in *anticipate*, *antipathy*, *antilogy* (against speaking), and *antilopine* (bet you didn't know that word, which means "pertaining to antelopes"; neither did we, but, like the others, it's usually pronounced with the stress on that second syllable)—thus "an-TIP-uh-deez."

And if *antipodes* sounds like a plural to you, you're correct. Is there a singular *antipode*? Well, technically, yes . . . and it *is* pronounced "anti-PODE," but it is very rarely used.

anyway

[EN-EE-way]

*anyhow, nonetheless, supports or refers
back to a previous statement or point*

What is this simple word doing in a collection of shibboleth words? Yes, of course you know how to pronounce this. Good for you . . . since an alarming number of people seem to think there is an *s* at the end of it. "Anyways," they say. "I was going to say it correctly anyways."

But it's *anyway*, singular, derived from the phrase "by any way" dating back to the 1300s. It's possible the errant *s* added to *anyways* stemmed from the Middle English *ani-gates* (somehow, in any way), since *any ways* has appeared in texts from about 1560. But it doesn't matter: no *s*, any and way. That's it—pure and simple.

armoire

[arm-WAHR]

cupboard

Armoire is one of those classic French words that people mispronounce probably thinking they're showing how educated they are by pronouncing it the French way. Knowing that you don't pronounce the final consonants in many French words, they lop off the *r* and pronounce it "arm-WAH." The problem is that when there's an *e* on the other side of the consonant in French, you typically don't pronounce the *e* but do pronounce the consonant: thus, "arm-WAHR."

Actually, if you really want to sound Gallic, you'll have to pronounce that final *r* differently: act like you're going to say an *r* with a guttural accent, but then sort of stop midway. This will approximate the French sound, a subtle *r*. But why bother? We never say *Paris* the French way—"pa-REE"—so why try it with *armoire*? We say stick with the quasi-French but acceptable and classy-enough English "arm-WAHR" and be happy . . . or, as the French say, *heureux*.

asterisk

[ASS-ter-isk]

star-shaped typographical symbol: *

People have been mispronouncing *asterisk* since the word entered the English language from late Latin (*asteriscus* from the ancient Greek *asterriskos,* meaning "little star.")

The problem here is switching the correct *sk* ending with a *ks* ending. (Some people take it a step further and drop the *s*.) If you do it or have done it, you are not alone. People have been switching letters and sounds in English (and other languages) since language began. It is called *metathesis*—the rearranging of sounds in a word. It's happened in the past with some very common English words. The stuff you mow on the front lawn was called *gaers* in Anglo-Saxon times until someone switched the *r* to the front of the word to make *grass*; and *birds* used to be called *brids*, and, of course, while we still say *three*, we don't say *threeteen*.

So mispronouncers of *asterisk* have a long history of metathesis behind them. That said, it *is* "ASS-ter-isk." But if you keep getting tongue-tied, you can always do what techie types do: they simply call an asterisk symbol a star (as in *C**, pronounced "CEE-star") or a splat, both very easy to pronounce—and very hard to mispronounce.

Augustine

[aw-GUS-tin]

philosopher and saint

A few years back, TV weatherman Al Roker mispronounced the Florida city of St. Augustine, and the whole city was talking. But he mispronounced it for all the right reasons.

Augustine, or more fully, Aurelius Augustinus Hipponensis, was a great ancient Latin Christian writer, philosopher, and theologian who gave his books and ideas to the world and his name to numerous colleges, high schools, seminaries, and, yes, that city in Florida. His name in English is pronounced "aw-GUS-tin," which is how Al Roker pronounced it. But the city of St. Augustine is the one major place in which the name is pronounced differently—"aw-gus-TEEN," probably because that city name came to English via its Spanish founders.

Actually, how to pronounce *Augustine* "correctly" is debatable. In Latin, it's *Augustinus* pronounced "ow-goost-EE-nus," with a stress or accent on the *ee*. But, although you'd think that would mean it should be properly pronounced "aw-gus-TEEN" in English, it isn't, due to complicated rules of accenting. (Maybe the British had a better idea: they had another St. Augustine, of Canterbury, whose name they often shortened to Austin as in the capital of Texas, and there's no debate about how to pronounce that. . . .)

badminton

[BAD-mint-en]

*racket game in which a lightweight
shuttlecock is hit across a net*

Badminton (not "bad-mitten") is named after Badminton
House, the Duke of Beaufort's estate in Gloucestershire
(pronounced, of course, "GLOSS-ter"). The first known
reference to the game as *badminton* is an 1860 booklet
entitled "Badminton Battledore—a new game."

You would assume, then, that Badminton House is where
the game originated . . . but you would be wrong. While it
was played there, badminton actually started in British India
when British officers added a net to the traditional game of
battledore and shuttlecock. As it was particularly popular in
the garrison town of Poona—in fact, that was where the first
official rules were written in 1873—the game was sometimes
called Poona.

But *Poona* as a name for the game didn't catch on.
Badminton did. As for Badminton House—its name evolved
from the Old English *Badimyncgtun*, which meant "the
estate of Baduhelm" (the person who owned it).

banal

[buh-NAL] (also [buh-NAHL], [BAY-null])

so lacking in originality as to be obvious and boring

In a recent survey, many people said they were afraid to use *banal* in a conversation because they were afraid they were pronouncing it incorrectly. They shouldn't have worried. Chances are that, however they were pronouncing it, it was fine since dictionaries in the United States commonly list not one but *three* acceptable pronunciations.

That said, we'd say go for pronouncing *banal* as loosely rhyming with *canal*—first, because most people already do (this pronunciation was preferred by 58 percent of the Usage Panel of the *American Heritage Dictionary* in their major language survey of 2001); and second, because when the word first originated, the late Romans pronounced it with an accent or emphasis on the second *a*. (We say *banal*. The Romans said *bannalis*; when they used the word, they meant mandatory work under feudal law, especially at mills, wells, and bakeries; which is what common folk did, and so eventually *bannalis*, with the *is* chopped off, just came to mean "commonplace or trite").

Beijing

[bay-JING]

capital of People's Republic of China

Beijing is mispronounced by almost all English speakers, including world travelers. They say "bay-ZHING" with the *j* sound as in "beige" instead the preferred hard *j* sound as in "jungle." Of course, it's very difficult for nonnative Mandarin Chinese speakers to intonate it correctly. The *j* is slightly different even from what we've just said. It is *unvoiced* (your throat shouldn't vibrate when you say it) unlike the *j* in "jungle." Experts say it's actually more like an *x* with a small stop that sounds similar to a *j*.

Confused yet? It's even more complicated. Because Mandarin Chinese is a tonal language, the syllables in *Beijing* have different tones. The "bei" part is low-falling; the tone "jing" is high and flat. It's difficult to describe. You really have to hear it. That's why we say "Never mind" and just go for the modern diplomatically used "j-as-in-jungle" sound, the now-preferred English pronunciation. Don't worry about tones and trying to sound even more Chinese. After all, we say *Moscow* not *Moskva*, and *Munich* not *Munchen*.

One note: Beijing-ers commonly refer to Beijing by its Roman letter initials, "BJ." Sometimes when writing to American friends, they may say things that sound awkward to American ears. Be warned.

boatswain

[BO-zun, BO-sun]

nautical title for the warrant or petty officer in charge of sails, rigging, anchors, cables, and so on, as well as all work on the deck of a ship

Boatswain is one of those words that many people (confession: us, at one time) read and, because the spelling is so straightforward, assume they know how to pronounce it. "Boat" and "swain"—what could be difficult about that?

Well . . . it's wrong. To pronounce *boatswain* correctly (as with other nautical terms—see *forecastle, coxswain*), you have to pretend you're an old salt on the deck of a ship too busy with the business of sailing to pronounce every syllable in a word. "Where's the blasted bosun? We've got a problem with the focsle!" If you're writing about the old salt, know that you can turn to alternatives—phonetic spellings of *boatswain* such as *bo'sun, bos'n,* and the very apostrophe-heavy *bo's'n*—to make things a little easier for your readers.

bouillon

[BOOL-yen] or [BOOL-yon] (with a very light *L* sound)

*clear meat or vegetable broth used
as a base for soups and stews*

Unless you're trying to make a 14K golden stew or sterling silver soup, bouillon should be pronounced as "BOO(L)-yon," with a very light *L* sound (*bullion*—"BULL-yan"—refers to gold or silver bars. However (and this is where word origins are fun), both *bouillon* and *bullion* in English come from the same French word, *bouillir* (to boil), or, more specifically, *bouillon* (boiling). In the case of the metal bullion, the boiling referred to is the molten metal used to make gold or silver bars. In the case of the soup bouillon, of course, it referred to boiling broth.

Just to be tricky, though, the French no longer typically say *bouillon* for their gold or silver bullion. They use the word *lingots*—which, when you think about it, should be familiar to English speakers who use the word *ingots*.

HOW TO SOUND LIKE YOU'RE FROM ACROSS THE POND

Eighteen British Names and Their Unexpected Pronunciations

Althorp: ALL-trup

Belvoir: BEE-ver

Cholmondely: CHUM-lee

Featherstonehaugh: FAN-shaw

Kirkby: KER-bee

Leicester: LESS-ter

Leominster: LEMS-ter

Leveson-Gower: LOO-sen–gaw

Loughborough: LUF-brah

Mainwaring: MAN-err-ing

Marjoribanks: MARCH-banks

Mousehole: MOW-zel

Ralph: rayf

Ranulph: ralph

St.-John: SIN-jin (but only when hyphenated)

Towcester: TOE-ster

Woolfardisworthy: WOOL-ser-ee

Wriothesley: ROX-lee

bruschetta

[broo-SKEH-tah]

Italian specialty antipasto—grilled bread with olive oil, garlic, tomatoes, salt, and pepper, sometimes also with cheese and other toppings.

Here's a food we've known and loved for years that we've always pronounced "broo-SHET-a"—and no one ever corrected us. Probably the waiters were too polite (or they didn't know either). In a survey of the most commonly mispronounced food words done by the *Chicago Tribune*, *bruschetta* easily made it into the top ten.

For the record, it's pronounced "broo-SKET-tah" with a hard *ch* sound, as in modern Italian. The word comes from the old Tuscan Italian dialect and is derived from the word *bruscare*, meaning "to roast over coals." And that word probably comes from the late Latin word *brusicare* (to burn), which suggests that this delicious dish was probably eaten as far back as in the days of Julius Caesar. Then it was a humble dish for farmers; a hunk of stale bread, moistened with a bit of water, toasted over a fire, and rubbed with olive oil and garlic (but no tomatoes—they didn't make it to Europe until the 1500s).

Quick tip for food snobs: If you want to sound truly knowledgeable and annoying, when ordering more than one bruschetta, use the correct plural—not *bruschettas*, but *bruschette*.

buck naked

[buck NAY-ked]

completely nude

"Buck naked" isn't in this collection because it's hard to pronounce (it isn't), but because many people instead say the more evocative "butt naked." (Here's a favorite recent example in print—the very apropos header for a news video: "Kim Kardashian Butt Naked for Paper Magazine.")

This is an example of what linguists call an "eggcorn," when someone twists a phrase or word, replacing all or part of it with a soundalike that actually makes some sense, like "*butt* naked" instead of "*buck* naked."

One theory says "butt naked" actually came first and that "buck naked" emerged as the polite euphemism. But it's nearly impossible to find printed examples of "butt naked" before the late 1960s, while the first printed use of "buck naked" appeared in 1928. What does the "buck" refer to? There are different theories, among them that it came from the word *buckskin*, from the slang used by Americans to refer derogatorily to young Native American and African American males, from the use of the slang term *bucket* for *buttocks*. Or perhaps it's simply that *butt* evolved into *buck*.

So "butt naked" might not really be far off the mark. But if you're a purist, stick with the "buck." It's the time-honored correct version. And there are no ifs, ands, or "butts" about it.

buoy

[boy, bwoy, or BOO-wee]

noun: an anchored floating object in water that shows hazards, mooring places, and so on; verb: to keep afloat; to mark with a buoy

This is a true shibboleth word in that how you pronounce this word depends a great deal on where you live. "Boy," "bwoy," and "BOO-wee" are all technically correct, although "boy" is the pronunciation that is most often found in dictionaries.

Buoy is first found in the fifteenth century—spelled *boye* or *boyee, bouee, boie, boya, boia, boei,* and *boia* depending upon the language (Old French, English, French, Norman, Spanish, Portuguese, Dutch, and Provençal, respectively). No one is sure whether the English *buoy* evolved from the Old French (*boye*) or Middle Dutch (*boei*). As for pronunciation, it's a split decision: linguists historically have recognized "bwoy" as the preferred pronunciation, but "boy" is more common among sailors (who should know best) and is more often found in England and other non-American English-speaking countries. It's the most common pronunciation in New England as well. As for the rest of the United States, "BOO-wee" wins. But to further complicate matters, those who say "BOO-wee" typically pronounce the "buoy" in *buoyant* and *buoyancy* as "boy."

It's enough to make one's spirits less than, well, buoyant.

cache

[cash]

a hiding place; anything hidden in the hiding place, often stolen or illegal (as in "a cache of jewelry" or "a cache of drugs"); goods stored that can be easily accessed when needed

Cache is one of those French-derived words that confuses many people. It looks like it is two syllables and, like its cousin *cachet*, the "che" looks like it could be pronounced "shay." However, it isn't.

Its first known use was in 1797 when French Canadian trappers used it to refer to their hiding places where they stored their furs and food. It evolved from the Old French *cachier* (to hide). By the 1830s, *cache* was also used to refer to hidden or stored goods. *Cachet*, on the other hand, comes from the same parents (*cachier* or, later, *cacher*)—the Latin *coactare*, meaning "to constrain or compel"—but in the sense of "pressing," not "hiding"; *cachet* evolved into a different word with a completely different meaning: the sixteenth-century French word meaning "seal affixed to a letter or document." (Perhaps this is the root of *cachet*'s current meaning of carrying prestige.)

In closing, let us simply say that it takes cachet to pronounce *cache* correctly. Okay, now that we've gotten that out of our system. . . .

Celtic

[KEL-tic] (for most usages),
[SEL-tic] (for the Boston and Glasgow sports teams)

of or belonging to the Celts; speakers of languages in parts of Britain, France, and Ireland; languages Breton, Welsh, Irish, Manx, Scots Gaelic, Cornish, and so on.

"KEL-tic," "SELtic" . . . either way is fine in general. But most Celtic Studies scholars and students say "KEL-tic" when referring to things Irish, Gaelic, or the like, and *all* sports fans say "SEL-tic" when referring to their beloved Boston basketball team ("Selts" is also okay) or the Glaswegian football team, the Celtic F. C.

Celtic comes from the Greek word for the group of people who lived along the Danube and Rhone Rivers, whom they called the Keltoi. Many of them migrated westward and so did the words referring to them. *Keltoi* became, in Latin, *Celtae,* and the adjective referring to them, *Celticus* (both still pronounced with an opening *k* sound). They evolved into the French *Celtes* and *Celtique* (with a soft *c*) from which English derives *Celt* and *Celtic* (also initially pronounced with a soft *c*). But after the 1600s, classical scholars reintroduced the ancient pronunciation, and gradually it caught on with nonacademics as well, so the hard *k* it generally is. But never, ever go to Boston and cheer the "Kelts"!

chaise longue

[shays LAWHN(g)] (just a hint of a *g*)

long, low chair with a back along half its length and one arm; reclining long chair

Yes, as you can see above, it is not "chaise lounge." But if you thought it was, you're far from alone. A highly unscientific survey (which consisted of typing "chaise lounge" into Google) proves this. The incorrect term occurred over one million times—including in listings for stores like Ikea, Walmart, Home Depot, and Amazon. Granted, the correct spelling shows up over two million times, but over one million incidences of an incorrect word is quite impressive.

It is clearly an easy mistake to make, and it has been made since the word emerged in the early 1800s. But the word *chaise longue* means, literally, "long chair" in French, not "lounge chair." The piece of furniture itself has been around for centuries, first made in ancient Egypt by lashing palm sticks together with rawhide. They were also widely used in ancient Greece and, later, Rome. So the furniture has a long (*longue*?) history.

One note: While "*shays LAWHNg*" is the correct pronunciation, use it only if you're French or trying to sound French or letting people know that is how it is technically pronounced. Otherwise, we give you permission to stick with plain old "chaise lounge."

champ at the bit

[champ at the bit]

to be impatient while being delayed

At the Kentucky Derby just before the race, there are many horses champing (not chomping) at the bit. *Champing* means chewing or grinding noisily, so a horse champing at the bit is a horse worrying the bit in his mouth because he is anxious for the race to start.

This idiom or phrase has been around at least since 1577 and is now usually applied to humans who are extremely eager to do something. But most people say *chomping* at the bit . . . probably because *champing* is such an uncommon verb. The British blame this on the Americans, who apparently began substituting "chomp" for "champ" in a big way back in the 1930s. Some writers claim it was even earlier than that, back in the 1800s.

Even though it's not considered correct, a quick Google search shows that *chomp at the bit* is twice as common as the "champ" phrase, and a recent survey found that in American published books and newspapers *chomped* is outrunning *champed* in this linguistic race. Which word is going to win? Ultimately, it doesn't really matter as dictionaries like *Merriam-Webster* accept both versions as correct, although we prefer the older *champ*.

chiaroscuro

[kee-ahr-uh-SKYOOR-oh]

*in art, the treatment of light and shade,
often in dramatic contrast*

A little while back on some early morning show, the topic of Old Master paintings came up and the host stumbled not once but three times over this word that had popped up on the teleprompter. He began with an incorrect *ch* sound, then tripped over the "ia" and stumbled back to the "chia," now pronouncing it like the chia plant (aka unwanted Christmas gift). His host chimed in to help and then she completely mangled the word as well. They both ended up wondering what the word meant.

It wasn't surprising. *Chiaroscuro* looks odd, sounds odd, and just doesn't crop up in everyday conversation since it basically refers to the artistic technique of balancing dark and light, the interplay of light and shadow. It came into English from the Italian and is still pronounced the Italian way, with *chiaro* (clear, bright) joined to *oscuro*, (obscure, dark). But to pronounce it correctly, it's easier to think of four English words set in a row: "key arrow skew row."

chimera

[ky-MEE-rah]

an illusion of the mind; originally a Greek mythological monster with lion's head, goat's body, and snake's tail; in biology, an organism or tissue consisting of different genetic parts, such as a tomato with fish genes

The movie *Mission: Impossible II* featured the deadly chimera virus, where it was pronounced correctly, with a hard *k* sound for *ch*. For many people, that film was a pronunciation eye-opener: they'd previously said "chi-MER-a" or "shi-MER-a" instead of "ky-MEE-rah" (although we doubt they used the word that often).

Chimera (like *chameleon*, also with an opening *k* sound) comes from the ancient Greek, and the *ch* you see represents the Greek letter *chi* (which in Greek looks something like a large X.) It sounded something like a *k* sound followed by a puff of air.

When the Romans took the word into Latin, they didn't have a *chi* letter and their *c* was already being used, so they represented the sound with *ch*. Since they also didn't have the Greek *chi* sound, they pronounced it as a *k*. That's the source of the confusion when they passed the word on to the French and then on to the English, who saw the *ch* and pronounced it as they would commonly do in their own languages. In a sense *chimera*, in terms of its combined pronunciation, can be said to be a linguistic chimera!

chiton

[KITE-un]

ancient Greek tunic; mollusk with a boat-shaped shell

Chiton is not one of those words that crops up in everyday conversation unless you're a classics scholar or—here's a word you also rarely hear—a malacologist (a biologist specializing in mollusks).

But if by chance you need to use the word, remember that, like *chimera*, *chiton* came to English via Latin from the ancient Greeks and the *ch* should be pronounced with the classical *k* sound. (Somewhat confusingly, by the time of late Rome, a true *ch* sound did occur in Latin, only it wasn't represented by a *ch*: *c* followed by an *e, ae, oe, i,* or *y* came to be pronounced like the *ch* in church, so *Cecilia* was pronounced "che-CHEE-lee-a," while *ch* was still pronounced *k*!)

The word *chiton* apparently came from the oldest civilizations of the Fertile Crescent via the Sumerian word for flax (*gada*) or linen (*gida*), which became the Akkadian *kittan*. Take note: A similar word, with the same origins, *chitin*, the hard substance that makes up insect and other arthropod exoskeletons, is also pronounced with a *k*. Now you can toss these words around at your next malacological or entomological party.

chutzpah

[kHUT-spa] or [kHOOT-spa] (with a slightly aspirated *kh*)

nerve, gall, audacity

If you're Jewish (or from New York or Los Angeles), you probably wouldn't think of this as a shibboleth word. But for many people—especially those who say "CHUT-spa" or "CHOOTS-pah"—*chutzpah* is Greek to them. Well, Yiddish. . . .

It is a word with very old roots, coming from the Aramaic *hu spa* to the Hebrew *hutspah* (gall or impudence), which became the Yiddish *khutspe* and, finally, *chutzpah*. It was initially used more as a bit of a pejorative (in the sense of excessive nerve or gall) but has become more celebratory, applied to enviable ballsiness.

Perhaps the best explanation of how to pronounce it is this one from Leo Rosten in *The Joys of Yiddish*: "Rattle the *kh* around with fervor; rhymes with *foot spa*. Pronounce the *ch* not as in 'choo choo' or 'Chippewa,' but as the German *ch* in 'Ach!' or the Scottish in loch."

claddagh

[KLAH-dah]

a symbol representing friendship, love, and loyalty, consisting of two hands holding a crowned heart (the hands represent friendship, the heart love, and the crown loyalty); usually found on a ring

Claddagh is one of those words that you might hesitate to pronounce because so many Irish Gaelic-based words are spelled in ways that bear little resemblance to their sound . . . like *Niamh*, pronounced "NEE-ov," or *Tadgh*, pronounced "tig." Happily, though, *claddagh* isn't as tough as many of its cultural relatives. It's almost the way it is spelled, just without a hard *g* or *gh* at the end: easy peasy or, rather, *éasca péasca*!

According to legend, the design of the claddagh—two hands holding a heart—came about when Richard Joyce was kidnapped while at sea and sold to a Moorish goldsmith. Freed after fourteen years, he returned to Galway where his true love had waited for him and gave her the ring he had made during his enslavement. Is the story true? No one is sure, but his initials are inside one of the oldest claddagh rings.

What we do know for sure is that the claddagh ring was first produced in the early seventeenth century in an Irish fishing village near Galway that was not-so-surprisingly named Claddagh (or, in Irish, Chladaigh or Chladach)—and that it wasn't actually called a claddagh ring until the mid-1800s.

coitus

[KOH-i-tus]

sexual union, especially between a man and a woman

Coitus is a short word that, frankly, isn't used all that often in conversation, which might be a lucky thing, not because there's anything wrong with talking about sexual intercourse, but because so many people pronounce it incorrectly. Otherwise smart people wind up talking about "koh-EYE-tus" or "koh-EE-tus" or "KOY-tus," which is the way (fictional) theoretical physicist Dr. Sheldon Cooper on the *Big Bang Theory* says it. While he has a (fictional) PhD *and* SciD, he's no linguist.

Coitus is supposed to be three syllables, and the *i* is short, making the "coi" sound more like *coincidence* than *coin*. But as with so many other shibboleth words, the *wrong* pronunciation—the two-syllable version—is becoming more widely used. Perhaps we should blame (fictional) Dr. Cooper and his friends. . . .

The word comes from the Latin *coitus*, a meeting together or a sexual union; when it became part of English in the eighteenth century, it was initially used to mean "meeting" or "uniting." But now it is only used to mean sexual intercourse. (If you try using it to mean "meeting," even if you pronounce it the preferred way, we suspect people will look rather oddly at you.)

comptroller

[con-TROLL-er]

*a management-level position responsible for
supervising the quality of accounting and
financial reporting of an organization*

This incredibly annoying word has been bothering people
since the early 1500s. In spite of its rather straightforward
spelling, it technically is pronounced "*con*-TROLL-er"
rather than "*comp*-TROLL-er. So why such a disconnect . . .
and what happened to the *mp*?

The word actually comes from the Middle English
countreroller (a person who checks a scroll copy) via the
French *contreroule* (a scroll copy or counter-roll) . . . and is
really *controller* (a word that is used interchangeably with
comptroller). But somehow, somewhere, someone thought
that the word evolved from the French *compte* (an account),
which led to misspelling *controller* as *comptroller*, even
while keeping the original (correct) pronunciation.

Note: Because so many people have mispronounced
this word for so many years, pronouncing it the way it is
spelled (i.e., with the *mp*) is becoming acceptable, even
if not technically correct.

corpsman

[COR-muhn] or, less commonly,
[CORZ-muhn] (with just a slight *z* sound)

enlisted service personnel, often medical

If you've always said "corpse man," join the club. It's one of the most commonly mispronounced words in the English language. Even U.S. President Barack Obama mispronounced this word referring three times to a "corpse man" at an annual National Prayer Breakfast.

The problem is that the "corps" part of the word came into English from the French—and many words in French don't sound out some final consonants. In this case, *corps* (body), is pronounced "core" (or sometimes "corz" with just a hint of a *z*), with no *p* sound at the end of the word.

Corps originally came from the Latin *corpus*, in which the *p* is pronounced. Both *corps* and *corpse* are intertwined historically—they were virtually the same word until recently (*corpse* was spelled *corps* until the 1800s) and they share that same Latin parent, *corpus*. It's just that the *p* sound is sounded in *corpse* and not in *corps*. Just to make things more confusing, *corpse* used to be pronounced without the *p* as well. The *p* was added by learned types to make it more like the original Latin.

HOW TO SOUND LIKE A FASHIONISTA

The Fashionable Way to Pronounce
Sixteen of the Top Fashion Names

Bulgari: BUHL-guh-ree

Chanel: shuh-NEL

Christian Lacroix: KRIS-tee-anh luh-KWA

Comme des Garçons: kohm day gar-SAW(n)
(with a soft *n*)

Givenchy: zhee-VON-she

Hermes: AIR-mehz

Louboutin: loo-boo-TAH(n) (with a soft *n*)

Louis Vuitton: LOO-ee VWEE-tah(n) (with a soft *n*)

Maison Martin Margiela: MAYZ-on Mar-TIN mar-ZHEL-a

Manolo Blahnik: muh-NO-low BLAH-nik

Miu Miu: mew mew

Proenza Schouler: pro-EN-za SKOOL-er

Ralph Lauren: ralf LOR-uhn
(This should be easy, but many people say "lor-EN")

Versace: ver-SAH-chay

Yves Saint Laurent: eev sahn LOR-uhn
(with a nasal "sahn")

Zegna: ZAYN-yah

coup de grâce

[coo-de-GRAHS]

finishing blow

Kill Bill: Volume 2 pronounced it "coo-de-GRAH" (twice); so did a Steely Dan song, and so do many people. Are they right? *Non.* The ending *s* sound must be pronounced.

Coup de grâce in French literally means "stroke of grace," as in giving a merciful sword blow to put a mortally wounded enemy soldier or condemned criminal out of his or her misery. But when it's pronounced "coo-de-GRAH," it would be written in French as *coup de gras*, which means "a stroke of grease or fat" . . . something most people probably don't wish to invoke.

This is an example of a *hyperforeignism*, when people try too hard to make a word that's been imported into English more like the foreign language it came from. In this case, people who know a little French (but not enough) know that final consonants are often dropped in French. So they're off and running, dropping those sounds willy-nilly. They're right with the *p* in *coup* but they're wrong with that *c*.

So next time you hear someone intoning about a final "coo-de-GRAH"—unless they're a chef with a pot full of lard literally or figuratively about to finish off someone with a large dollop of fat—you'll realize they're mispronouncing this very commonly mispronounced phrase.

coxswain

[COCK-suhn]

the person in charge of (and typically the one who steers) a ship's s mall boat; in a racing shell, the person who calls orders to the rowers

Welcome back to the wonderful world of nautical pronunciation in which words are mumbled, slurred, and otherwise transmogrified into something only vaguely resembling the spelling! Here is another example of elision (see *boatswain*) in which one or more sounds (in this case, the long *a* in *swain*) are omitted.

Coxswain evolved from the Middle English melding of the words *cok* (cockboat—a small boat) and *swain* (servant). Initially it was spelled with a *k* instead of an *x*, but there were other variations on the theme—*cokswain, cockswayne,* and even *kokeswayne*.

Over time, there were numerous other spellings as well, usually incorporating the *x* and sometimes actually closer to the actual pronunciation of the word. Samuel Pepys in his famous diaries wrote of the Coxon of the Vice-Admirall (yes, he spelled admiral a bit differently as well). And *coxen* was listed as an alternative spelling in the 1769 *Universal Dictionary Marine*. But these blessedly reasonable spellings didn't catch on. By the nineteenth century, *coxswain* became the go-to if nonphonetic spelling . . . and thus it remains.

croissant

[kwah-SAHNT] (or [kwah-SAHWN],
with a soft French *n*)

*a French crescent-shaped buttery roll,
usually eaten at breakfast*

Many foodies face a dilemma when ordering a croissant—
the French word for the flakey, buttery, crescent-shaped
roll (and the word for "crescent" as well). Should they go all
French and pronounce it as the French do (or at least try)—
with a gutteral *r* almost like clearing your throat and then,
of course, with the classic French nasal *n* ending? Or should
they take the middle course and opt for "kwah-SAHNT"?
Or should they go all-American and say "cross-ANT" . . .
which will probably only garner stares? We suggest the
middle one: "kwah-SAHNT." At least you're trying, but not
to a ridiculous degree.

One quick note on origins: Although many food sources
romantically state that croissants were developed to
celebrate the defeat of Turks invading Europe (Muslims
used the crescent shape on their flags), the consensus now
is more prosaic. In 1839, an Austrian officer August Zang
opened a Viennese bakery (Boulangerie Viennoise) in Paris.
He served a crescent-shaped Austrian pastry, *kipferl*, the
origins of which go back to the 1300s, and which soon had
thousands of French imitators. *Kipferl* meant "moon" or
"crescent," but of course the French preferred using their
word, and so the French croissant was born.

crudités

[kroo-de-TAY]

*raw vegetables usually cut into bite-sized pieces
and served with dipping sauce as an hors d'oeuvre*

This word entered English-speakers' vocabularies in the twentieth century when the notion of raw veggies arranged nicely on a plate around a cup of ranch dressing became accepted as the height of sophisticated cocktail party food. The *Oxford English Dictionary* (*OED*) notes that it appears as early as 1960 in cookbooks, but the real surge in popularity, when every magazine offered tips for a crudités plate, was in the later 1960s. The word itself is quite old, coming from the fourteenth-century French word *crudité* (rawness or, of course, crudity), which in turn came from the Latin *crudus* (raw or rough).

And you would be giving this word a raw deal if you Americanized it and said, as many do, "KROO-dites" or "KROO-de-tees" or, perhaps the least appetizing, "KRUD-ites." Because it's French and has kept most of its original pronunciation intact, the *é* has the typical French *ay* sound. Most dictionaries list this as a plural word—implying by omission that there's no such thing as a *crudité*—but say that it can be used with either a singular or plural verb. But in the food world, the singular *crudité* is used.

Cthulhu

[KHLULL-hloo]

*part man, dragon, octopus, fictional deity,
created by writer H. P. Lovecraft*

Cthulhu burst onto the dark science fiction/fantasy scene in 1928, in Lovecraft's short story "The Call of Cthulhu" and since then has become a cult figure, turning up in computer games, TV shows, and Internet memes. It's a name you've probably seen, but never really tried to deal with out loud. *Cthooloohoo*? *Cathullhue*? Actually, we're all forgiven if we can't pronounce *Cthulhu* correctly, since its creator H. P. Lovecraft himself said that humans aren't physically able to do so. He made a stab at explaining how to get close in a 1934 letter to friend and fellow writer Duane W. Rimel:

> *The actual sound—as nearly as human organs could imitate it or human letters record it—may be taken as something like "Khlûl'-hloo," with the first syllable pronounced gutturally and very thickly. The u is about like that in "full"; and the first syllable is not unlike "klul" in sound, since the h represents the guttural thickness. The second syllable is not very well rendered—the l sound being unrepresented.*

Well, that (kind of) clears things up. . . .

cumin

[COO-min], [KYOO-min], or [CUH-min]

spice, used often in Indian and Mexican food

Cumin is a spice with an identity problem. It is most frequently pronounced "COO-min," but dictionaries also include "KYOO-min," and "CUM-min"—as in, "Come in and tell me how to pronounce this annoying word." Until very recently, this latter pronunciation was the only one listed in most dictionaries. But just as more people began using the spice itself, so too more people began saying it with either the long *u* ("COO") or with what's called a *y-glide* ("KYOO"), so lexicographers added these pronunciations, some even making the alternatives the preferred way to say *cumin, . . .* which is where we are now.

Cumin comes from the Old English *cymen,* by way of the Latin *cuminum,* which was from the Greek *kuminon*—which probably evolved from the Semitic languages: Hebrew's *kammon* and Arabic's *kammun.* It has been spelled numerous ways including *commin, comin(e), comeyn, cummyn,* and *comyn*—none of which seem like they'd have the "KYOO" sound at all. And that makes us wonder about the "COO" as well. So which is right? Since variety is the spice of life, let's just let them coexist, although personally we're in the "COO-min" camp.

dais

[DAY-iss]

*platform, as in a lecture hall, for speakers
or honored guests*

Many people make this a one-syllable word—"dayss"—and for a long time, that's just how it was pronounced. But in American English, it is actually two syllables—"DAY-iss," which sounds a bit like "discus," which just happens to be the word it evolved from.

Discus was the Roman word for a disk-shaped object (from the Greek *diskos*). By late medieval times, it also referred to flat surfaces in general, then a table, and then a high table at the end of a hall where kings sat. By the time *discus* had come to France, it had lost the *c* and was one syllable—*deis* or *dois*. It crossed over to the British Isles as one syllable, *deys* or *des,* but it wasn't a popular word, except in Scotland, and soon died out in the 1600s. But two hundred years later, scholars with a penchant for it revived it. *Dais*'s first modern appearance in an English dictionary was only in 1846. Soon it gained in popularity, and the single syllable became two, which is how it remains.

Daylight Saving Time

[DAY-lite SAVE-ing time]

*when clocks are advanced during summer months
by one hour so that in the evening hours daylight
is experienced later*

Why did we include this common phrase? Because, well, think about it and be honest—do you say "Daylight Saving Time" or "Daylight *Savings* Time"? Many of us (we plead guilty) carelessly use the plural "savings," including the writer of a quite recent *Huffington Post* article, with the headline "Daylight Savings Time Starts March 8." Wrong.

It's "Daylight *Saving* Time." It's an easy mistake to make, probably because of the associations with common terms like *savings bank* and *savings account*. The British have a better idea. Often instead of calling it "Daylight Saving Time," a rather unwieldy phrase, they call it "Summer Time," which not only is a perfect opposite to "Standard Time" (non–daylight saving time) but also sounds so evocative.

desultory

[DES-ul-tory], also [DEZ-ul-tory]

*not having a plan or purpose, skipping about,
going aimlessly from one thing to another*

It is tempting to pronounce it otherwise, but with *desultory*, the accent is on the first syllable. For some reason, to many ears de-SUL-tory sounds classier and quasi-British. It also sounds *right* probably because of its similarity to common words like "insulting," which of course has a stress on the second syllable. But when it comes to *desultory*, it's very, very wrong!

Desultory comes from the circus . . . more specifically, from the Latin *dēsultōrius,* meaning "leaping." *Desultors* were Roman circus riders who leaped from one galloping horse to another; usually two horses at the same time, sitting on them without a saddle, and vaulting upon either of the horses to the roar of the crowd. Hence the modern usage of "jumping around from one idea to another," although certainly not at all in that vigorous circus horseback-riding sense. You are now allowed to be slow and desultory.

detritus

[de-TRY-tuss]

*waste, rubble, fragments broken off the
whole due to erosion, remains*

One of our favorite definitions of this word (because of
the breathtaking honesty) is found online in the *Urban
Dictionary*. "Stuff left behind, shit that no one wants. From
Latin. Often used when the speaker expects that the listener
won't know what the word means." We can attest to this.

Our confession: We've included this word since both of us
pronounced it incorrectly while using it frequently and, we
thought, impressively. "DEH-trit-uss," we said blithely. Now
we know better. We have left that pronunciation behind,
detritus of our ignorance, if you will.

It's possible that we and all those other people who
mispronounce this word do so because it seems similar to
detriment, which has the stress on the first syllable. And,
in fairness to us, *detriment* and *detritus* do share the same
root—the Latin *deterere* (to rub or wear away). But while
detriment evolved from the French *detriment* (complete
with accent on the first syllable) via the Latin *deterimentum*,
detritus came directly from the Latin *detritus*. Initially, it was
a geoscientific word, referring to erosion and the resulting
particulate. From this technical meaning has grown a
nontechnical one. *Detritus* now also refers more generally
to miscellaneous remnants and odds and ends.

diaeresis (also dieresis)

[dye-AIR-uh-sis]

*the separate pronunciation of a vowel in a diphthong,
sometimes marked by a (¨) placed over a vowel; in poetry,
a natural rhythmic break in a line of verse*

Diaeresis, which comes from the ancient Greek meaning
"to take apart," is best known as those two funny dots placed
over words like *naïve* to indicate two separate vowel sounds
or, on occasion, to indicate that a vowel must be pronounced
in a particular way, as in *Brontë*.

It's useful as a pronunciation tool. For example, *zoölogy*
with a diaeresis clearly shows that the first syllable isn't
pronounced "zoo" but "zoh-oh." But for better or worse, the
diaeresis is on its way out, replaced by a hyphen (*co-op*), or
nothing (*reelect*). Other than in classical poetic circles, this
word is rarely encountered or particularly needed. In fact,
the formidable Fowler of *Fowler's Modern English Usage*
says that the diaeresis "is in English an obsolescent symbol."

But for the glorious word snobs among us, it's vital not
to mispronounce words that so readily demonstrate our
literary prowess. Just think of it as "die heiresses" without
the *h*. (And now, a bit of literary trivia: *Brontë* was at one time
spelled without a diaeresis. Originally the Irish *Ó Proinntigh*,
it was anglicized as *Prunty* and sometimes *Brunty*. The Brontë
sisters' father, Patrick Brunty, changed it to *Brontë* with a
diaeresis over the *e* to indicate it should be pronounced "ay.")

diaspora

[dye-ASS-poh-rah]

dispersion, usually of peoples,
as of the Jews after leaving Israel

Diaspora comes from two ancient Greek words—*dia* (across)
and *spora* (scattered). It came into use further west via
translations of the Greek Bible, specifically from a section
of the book of Deuteronomy about Jews after the Captivity.
From there, the word entered English.

But even though it's all Greek, we don't pronounce the
word like the Greeks did. They pronounced it "di-ass-poh-
RAH." But we pronounce it "dye-ASS-poh-rah." You may
ask why. But do you *really* want to know about short,
penultimate (next to last) vowels in ancient Greek and
corresponding antepenultimate (before the next to last)
English stressed vowels, probably due to Latin rules applied
to Greek words in English? Probably not, but that's the
most likely reason. Just think of other words we pronounce
similarly—like *diaphanous* and *dialysis*, both from Greek
words, with the same "dia" and the same stress on the
a syllable following the *d*. One caveat: If by chance you
encounter a diasporometer (a scientific instrument for
measuring dispersion of light rays), pronounce it like this:
dye-ass-poh-ROM-meter.

Don Juan

[don JEW-ahn]

main character in Lord Byron's satiric poem

If, when talking about Lord Byron, you say, "I've always enjoyed his 'don JEW-ahn,'" most people will probably correct you ("It's 'don whan.'"). But you will be correct. Of course, if you are talking about *Don Juan* in any other context, it's plain old "whan" as usual. "JEW-ahn" is specifically applicable to Byron's character. But why is this *juan*, er, juan of a kind? (Forgive us.)

It's because Byron wrote the poem so that foreign words would be pronounced in accordance with *English* pronunciation rules. Herewith is the perfect example in which you can see exactly how he intends *Juan* to be pronounced based on the rhyme scheme:

> *Till, after cloying the gazettes with cant,*
> *The age discovers he is not the true one;*
> *Of such as these I should not care to vaunt,*
> *I'll therefore take our ancient friend Don Juan.*

Yes, *Juan* rhymes with "true one." That said, it feels quite unorthodox to say and, when reading about the poem (the title or references to it or the main character), most people probably still think of it as regular old "don whan." Byron himself got around the whole "whan"/"jew-ahn" issue in his own way: he referred to the character as "Donny Johnny" in letters to friends when he was working on the poem.

Dr. Seuss

[DOK-ter soyss]

pen name for Theodor Geisel

We didn't know this one either . . . and had no clue that since we were kids, we've been pronouncing the good doctor's name incorrectly. But, yes, Theodor (that's another thing—with no *e* at the end of his first name) Geisel's pen name was his mother's maiden name and actually rhymes with *voice* rather than *moose*.

The American public, unfamiliar with the German name, went the phonetic route. "Soos," they called him, incorrectly. Alexander Lang, a college pal with whom he worked on the *Dartmouth Jack-O-Lantern,* commemorated this lapse on the part of the reading public in verse:

> *You're wrong as the deuce*
> *And you shouldn't rejoice*
> *If you're calling him Seuss.*
> *He pronounces it Soice (or Zoice).*

But Dr., er, Soice soon succumbed to public whim and opted for the anglicized version as well. Not only was "soos" simpler since that's what everyone was already calling him, but, as an added bonus, it rhymed with another famous children's book figure: Mother Goose.

draught

[draft]

*current of air, deep drink, depth of water needed
to float a ship, beer served from a keg or cask*

Blame it on the British. In America, we write "draught" as it sounds—*draft*—but the British have preserved their old way of spelling, and even here in North America, many bars and brewers (maybe to seem properly "old country") advertise "draught beer" as well. But Americans almost always write "draft" for nonbeery uses of draught, and even the British write "draft" for certain things (like drafting a paper).

But when *draught* pops up in English literature, many of us think it's a different word than *draft* and mispronounce it. For example, in the *Lord of the Rings*, J. R. R. Tolkien talks about potent *ent-draughts*, which we read as the wonderfully mysterious sounding "ent-draouts." Little did we know that they were properly called *ent-drafts*, like the Bud on tap at the local bar.

This pronunciation/spelling problem began with Old English. *Draught* comes from the Old English *dreaht* or *dræht*. You don't see an *f* sound anywhere, but that *h* you do see sounds like a soft *ch* sound, as in Scots dialect *loch*. Over the centuries, this *ch* transmogrified into an *f* sound (for complex linguistic reasons of consonantal—not continental—drift), and the spelling changed. Isn't that a laugh . . . or should we write "laf"?

HOW TO SOUND WELL READ

Pronouncing Eighteen Writers' Names the Right Way

Chinua Achebe: CHIN-oo-ah ah-CHAY-bay

Donald/Frederick Barthelme: DON-ald/FRED-rik
BART-ell-mee or BART-uhl-mee

Roland Barthes: ROW-land bart

Catullus: cat-TULL-uss

Ta-Nehisi Coates: tah-nuh-HAH-see cotes

J. M. Coetzee: j m koot-ZEE-uh

Paulo Coelho: POW-loh kuh-WHEYL-oh

William Cowper: WIL-yam KOO-per

André Gide: AHN-dray zheed

Matt Groening: matt GRAY-ning

Milan Kundera: MEE-lahn koon-DER-uh

Jonathan Lethem: JON-uh-thun LEETH-em

Somerset Maugham: SUH-mer-set mawm

Anaïs Nin: ah-nayh-EES nin

Chuck Palahniuk: chuk PAHL-uh-nik

Jodi Picoult: joh-dee PEE-koh

Theodore Roethke: THEE-oh-dor RET-key

Evelyn Waugh: EEV-lin wah

dull as ditch water

[dull as dich WAW-ter]

exceptionally dull or boring

For most of us, it's easier to picture dishwater than ditch water, and that's probably the reason that "dull as dishwater" came about. But the phrase is technically "ditch water," although most dictionaries now say both are acceptable.

In the earliest uses of *ditch water* in a phrase, it meant "stuck up," as in *Pierce the Plowman's Crede* from 1394 or so: "digne as dich water" (*digne* meant "dignified"). But by the 1700s, *ditch* and *dull* joined hands, and "dull as ditch water" was commonly used and continued to be used for the next two hundred years.

As for *dishwater*, by itself it is an old term. We find "dysshe water" in a 1484 translation of Aesop's fables, phrases like "flat as dishwater" in 1781, and "dead as dishwater" in 1831. But there was no "dull as" until a bit later in the 1800s (1854, to be exact, in an appropriately boring story, "The Betrothal"). Even so, most Americans stuck with "dull as ditch water" until the latter part of the twentieth century when for some reason "dishwater" simply took off.

Of course, it seems silly to argue over which type of stagnant water is best suited to describe someone or something's excessive dullness. In fact, to go on would be as dull as . . . whichever.

electoral

[ee-LECK-tor-uhl]

relating to, or composed of, electors

We've all heard of the electoral college, that unwieldy process of choosing the president of the United States. But not only do many of us not understand how it works, we don't even pronounce it correctly. In fact, during election coverage, many newscasters who should know better seem to make a habit of mispronouncing it. They're not alone. Numerous websites and dictionaries put *electoral* among the top one hundred most mispronounced words in the English language. For the record, the accent is on the second syllable, not the third, so it's "ee-LECK-tor-uhl," not "ee-leck-TOR-uhl," and most definitely not "ee-leck-TOR-ee-uhl," which we've also heard.

Having said that, it's time for a caveat. *Merriam-Webster's Collegiate Dictionary* (11th edition), which tends to have a more liberal "go with the flow" attitude toward language than most other dictionaries, now accepts that second pronunciation and even adds a third "ih-LEK-trul" pronunciation. As a bonus political shibboleth word, as *electoral* goes, so goes *mayoral*. The "best" pronunciation is "MAY-or-uhl," but the mostly American alternate pronunciation "may-OR-uhl" is now acceptable as well. Now if you are campaigning to become a political sophisticate, we'd vote for the traditional pronunciations.

endive

[EN-dive or ahn-DEEV]

*a green, leafy vegetable from the daisy family
related to chicory, or the cream-colored
torpedo-shaped cultivated vegetable*

Many of us have wondered how to correctly pronounce
endive. Do you say it as it's spelled . . . or as if you're
pretending to be French? Surprisingly (well, to us),
they're *both* correct. It just depends on what type of
endive you're talking about.

The one properly pronounced "EN-dive" (*Cichorium
endivia*, to be technical) is a leafy, curly green vegetable
that grows naturally and is related to chicory and radicchio,
either curly endive (also known as *frisee)* and broad-leaf
endive (*escarole*).

Then there's the "ahn-DEEV" endive, the Belgian endive,
which is the one you probably run across most often on a
menu. It has a head of cream-colored tight leaves and is
cultivated from common chicory (*Cichorium intybus*), which
is, of course, a relative of the "EN-dive" endive. Belgian
endives are cultivated in a labor-intensive method that
entails keeping the plants completely away from sunlight.
They're called "Belgian" because the growing technique
originated in, yes, Belgium in the 1850s, although now
France is the largest producer of this type of endive. But
it's still not a French "ahn-DEEV."

et cetera

[et SET-er-uh]

*also, and so on, and so forth, and the rest,
and others; abbreviated as* etc.

It's not unusual to hear *et cetera* pronounced "eck SET-er-uh" and "ex SET-er-uh." Why do people do it? They're simply following a natural linguistic process known as *assimilation*, where sounds merge together and thereby become easier to pronounce. That of course doesn't make "eck-/ex SET-er-uh" correct.

It is formed from two Latin words—*et* (and) and *cetera* (the rest), so combined they are "and the rest." Both the *t* and the *c* must be pronounced, although the ancient Romans would have said the *c* with a hard *k* sound.

If you really want to dazzle people with your erudition but pronouncing *et cetera* correctly isn't enough for you, there is a similar Latin phrase that you can often substitute: *hoc genus omne*, sometimes with an "et" tacked to the front, as in "et hoc genus omne," which means "all that sort of thing." It has been used by such great writers of English as Lord Chesterfield and George Bernard Shaw, but maybe only they could get away with it. For the rest of us, we'd advise sticking with *et cetera* . . . pronounced without a *k* or *x*, of course.

flautist

[FLOU-tist]

person who plays the flute

This is actually a trick shibboleth because the word *flautist* is indeed real and is pronounced the way you probably assume it is. But while the term is used widely in Britain, in the United States, *flutist,* pronounced as it is spelled (FLOO-tist), is preferred.

While you might think *flutist* is simply an American evolution of *flautist*, it isn't. It's actually the older of the two—emerging in 1603, while *flautist* didn't come around until 1860, first appearing in Nathaniel Hawthorne's *The Magic Faun.* It's possible Hawthorne chose *flautist* because the book was set in Italy, where *flute* is *flauto* and a *flutist* is a *flautista. Flutist*, on the other hand, is a direct offspring of the French *flûtiste*, which came from *flûte.* So *flutist* has the historical claim and the more direct genealogy. Even so, many Americans persist in thinking *flautist* sounds more correct, more sophisticated, and more musical.

Our advice: Take the easy way out. Go with "flute player." As renowned musician James Galway put it: "I am a flute player, not a flautist. I don't have a flaut, and I've never flauted."

foliage

[FOH-lee-ij]

green leaves; collectively, greenery

Mispronouncers of *foliage* are guilty of the linguistic misdemeanor of metathesis (see *asterisk* on page 15). They switch the sounds in a word (in this case the *l* and the *i*, probably because "age" is a very common ending in English, and "iage" isn't. So "foliage" *sounds* right, even if it's wrong. A quick survey on a Scrabble word-ending dictionary found 411 English words ending in "age" and only 13 in "iage"—and several of those "iage" words, like *premarriage* and *remarriage*, are just variations of *marriage* so really don't count.

Foliage actually comes from a non-"iage" past, derived from the Old French word *feuillage*, from *feuille* (leaf). So how did the *i* switch places with the *l* and what about the *eu* changing too? It is probably due to a *back formation*, when scholars go back to the roots, in this case Latin, for the older, more "correct" formation of the word. Since the Latin for *leaf* is *folium*, you can immediately see where the *o* and the *i* probably came from.

If you're still having problems saying *foliage* correctly, you can always go back to Old English and say *berbene* or *þúfbære* instead—two other words that mean "foliage." Even if you mispronounce them, who's going to know?

for all intents and purposes

[for all intents and purposes]

essentially, for all practical purposes

The phrase is "for all intents and purposes," but many people instead say "for all intensive purposes." This is what's called an *eggcorn*, a soundalike stand-in for the correct word or phrase. And while it sounds similar, it is clearly wrong, something you can see if you examine the words. *Intensive* is an adjective meaning "vigorous or exhaustive." *Intents* is a noun meaning "purpose." They are obviously not interchangeable.

"For all intents and purposes" was originally a legal phrase. The earliest known use comes from an act adopted under King Henry VIII in 1547—"to all intents, constructions, and purposes." Probably because it sounded authoritative and all-encompassing, it quickly entered into English as a general phrase. The "constructions" in the phrase was omitted very early, and *for* was frequently substituted for *to*.

But there was never any proper use of *intensive* in this popular phrase, although some literary archaeologists have found it misused as early as the 1800s.

Putting aside its misuse, even correctly using this phrase is often frowned upon as an overused cliché by the more persnickety grammarian types. They point out that there are many simpler ways to say what the phrase means, like "essentially." And that is, for all intents and purposes, all you need to know.

forecastle

[FOHK-sul]

*the forward part of the main deck on a ship;
in merchant ships, sailors' under-deck living quarters*

Yet again, in *forecastle*, we meet a nautical word that looks
so nice and simple—*fore* and *castle*—what could be less
complicated? Pronounced with that old salt slur we've run
across in *boatswain* and *coxswain*, it's "FOHK-sul," not
"FORE-cass-el" and, also as with *boatswain*, it is sometimes
spelled the way it is pronounced—with apostrophes standing
in for the missing letters: *foc'sle, fo'c'sle*, or the apostrophe-
peppered *fo'c's'le*.

It is called a *forecastle* because until the later 1500s,
the deck at the fore of a ship was built on a higher level,
sometimes even with multilevels so that those on it could
shoot small arms and arrows at their enemy's ships. There
was also an *aftcastle*—an even bigger raised structure at the
aft of a ship. The unwieldy structures might have been assets
in battle, but they hampered the ship's maneuverability.
Once cannons became common in sea battles, the super-high
forecastles and aftcastles gave way to a lower, single-deck,
raised forecastle. Many modern ships don't even have a
legitimate forecastle, but the foredeck and crew's quarters
in the bow are still referred to as the *forecastle* . . . and keep
stumping landlubbers who read the word.

forte

[fort]

strength or talent; not the musical term for loud

Admission: This is a bit of a fake since *forte* is so widely pronounced as "for-TAY" that it has become acceptable. This is probably because there's another *forte*—pronounced "for-TAY"—that is a musical term meaning "loud." We're not talking about that word, but rather the other *forte*—meaning "strength" or "talent"—which is technically pronounced, yes, fort. That said, the distinguished Usage Panel of the *American Heritage Dictionary* preferred "for-TAY" by a ratio of three to one. But pedants still delight in saying "fort" and in correcting those who opt for the two-syllable pronunciation . . . and they are (technically) correct.

Both fortes came from the Latin word *fortis*, meaning "strong," but the musical term evolved through the Italian *forte*, pronounced "for-TAY," while the one-syllable *forte* evolved through the French word meaning "strong," *fort* (or the feminine *forte*) pronounced "FORT."

foyer

[FOY-er], [foy-YAY]

entrance hall

For many of us, foyer presents a difficult choice—whether to opt for the faux French version, "foy-YAY" or the plain old "FOY-yer." Which is correct? Answer: Both. "FOY-er" is more common in standard American English; "foy-YAY," in British and Canadian English. But there is spillover in both camps.

The "foy-YAY"/"FOY-er" split is common with words that were imported into English. Typically, they initially are pronounced more like the original language, but over time, they are anglicized and, often later, Americanized. In the case of *foyer*, it entered into English in 1859 (referring to a room in theater). The "foy-YAY" pronunciation is a partial anglicization of the French, since the first syllable would be more like "fwa." From that, it evolved into the more American "FOY-er," pronouncing it how it looks.

Usually you could guess that the later pronunciation would become the default and slowly push out the earlier one. *Foyer*, though, is a bit different because many Americans actually now think "foy-YAY" is more correct and are switching back to the Frenchier sound, thinking not only that it is right, but also that it is classier. (If you watch HGTV, you know what we mean. It's rare that an expensive house has a declassé "FOY-er.")

fungi

[FUN-guy]

plural of fungus

There's no debate about the singular pronunciation—it's "FUN-gus." But as for the plural, which uses the old original Latin *i* plural ending, there are many different so-called correct pronunciations. Many authors, grammarians, and blogs about words will confidently tell you to choose their one pronunciation, but then the next will confidently tell you the previous pronunciation is wrong. So what to do?

We suggest that you don't seek definitive help from dictionaries because you'll run across the same thing. They show numerous acceptable pronunciations in English, among them: "FUN-guy" (American and British), "FUN-jye" (American), "FUN-ghee" (American), "FUN-jee" (American), "fun-JEE" (American and British), and "fun-GHEE" (American and British). Forgive us if we have inadvertently omitted your favorite plural fungal pronunciation.

We tend to hear "FUN-guy" the most, especially around universities and scientists, so we recommend it. And when in doubt, you can also correctly use the English instead of the Latin plural (even though most scientists don't) and say "funguses" . . . or maybe just "mushrooms."

geoduck

[GOO-ee-duhk]

*a very large clam from the Pacific Northwest with a
siphon that can reach over three feet in length;
prized as a gourmet delicacy*

The original inhabitants of Puget Sound in the Pacific
Northwest, the Lushootseed or Coast Salish speakers, called
this very distinctive-looking clam a "GEWH-duhk." The
"uhk" part of the word apparently meant "genitals." Looking
at the long thick pumping siphon trunk of this big clam, we
can pretty easily guess what genitals the Coast Salish were
referring to. (Other more staid linguists suggest that the
word meant "dig deep" since the clams burrow very deep
into the mud.)

So why is it written "geoduck"? One theory has it that
English speakers in the 1800s most frequently wrote it as
"goeduck," which sounds fairly close to the Salish word. But
the "goe" part looked odd to American eyes, and gradually
the spelling was "corrected" into the more normal-looking
"geo." The *Oxford English Dictionary* primly omits the
possible genital origin, saying instead that the "duck" part of
the word referred to the siphon, which looks like the neck
of a dead duck. This sounds like stodgy etymology to us, but
dead ducks are probably gooey as well, so we'll give them
points for creativity.

GIF

[jiff]

computer graphic image; an acronym for
Graphics Interchange Format

Unlike its graphic counterpart the jpeg, which can only be pronounced like, well, "JAY-peg," the GIF is problematic. Is it "giff" with a hard *g* or "jiff" with a soft one?

Steve Wilhite says it's "jiff". . . and he should know since he developed GIFs for Compuserve. He chose to pronounce it that way because it sounded like Jif, the peanut butter brand. Employees would do a riff on Jif TV ads, saying, "Choosy developers choose GIF."

But choosy people who didn't develop the GIFs choose to say "giff" with a hard *g*. In fact, some dictionaries not only list both pronunciations, but place "giff" before "jiff."

Wilhite hasn't succumbed to pressure. When he got a lifetime achievement award back in 2013 at the Webby Awards, he gave a speech flatly rejecting "giff," which was widely shared on the Internet. So if you do choose the hard *g* version, we advise you to keep your mouth shut around Mr. Wilhite.

gnocchi

[NYAW-kee]

thick Italian soft-dough dumplings,
first-course alternative to soup

Eat24, an online food-delivery service, puts *gnocchi* in their top ten list of mispronounced food words. The problem is that the Italian *gn* has an *ny* sound. It shouldn't be that hard for us English speakers to say correctly, however. After all, the Italian *gn* sound is already familiar—most of us say *lasagna* correctly.

The problem with *gnocchi*, though, is that *gn* is at the beginning of the word, and in English, an initial *g* is usually silent (as in *gnome*); the *n* is sounded like normal English (except for *gnu*, which can be pronounced "nyu" but usually isn't).

Gnocchi, as you may have guessed, is plural. In the extremely unlikely event you want only one of these small foods, ask for a gnoccho; that's the singular. But that would be like asking for a strand of spaghetti. You'll probably get stares even if you do pronounce the singular correctly.

Goethe (Johann Wolfgang von)

[GE(r)-teh] (with just a hint of an r)

German writer and statesman (1749–1863), perhaps best known for his "sturm und drang" novel, The Sorrows of Young Werther, *and his epic,* Faust

You're expounding very eruditely about *Faust*, commenting on the parallels between selling one's soul and overindustrialization, and then you mention the writer's name: "Goath." At this point, anyone listening to you has forgotten your excellent literary points and is thinking you are a bit of a buffoon. (Note: This is a true story. The "you" shall remain nameless, but suffice it to say she is one of the authors of this book.)

It's "GER-te," sort of. The "ger" is specific to German—it's a hard *g* and the *er* is almost an *oe* (as in Oedipus) but with a hint of an *r*. In German, it was originally spelled *Göthe* with an umlaut over the *o*, which is often transliterated as *oe*. Goethe's grandfather switched to the umlaut-less spelling. You should pronounce the "goe" part of *Goethe* almost like an *eh* rather than an *oh;* the *r* sounds as though you are saying it while swallowing; and the "the" is a *t* with a tiny *eh* at the end.

The description is so complicated, you're almost forgiven if you stick with *Goath* (seriously? Of course not) . . . so we won't even mention how some Chicagoans pronounce Goethe Street. (Okay, we will: "GO-thee.")

HOW TO SOUND LIKE A SEASON TICKET HOLDER TO THE SYMPHONY

The Correct Way to Pronounce the Names of Eight Leading Composers

Claude Debussy: klohd duhb-yew-SEE

Antonin Dvorak: AHN-to-neen DVOR-zhahk

Sergei Prokofiev: SAYR-gay proh-KOH-fee-yef

Sergei Rachmaninoff: SAYR-gay rakh-MAWN-een-off

Nikolai Rimsky-Korsakov:
nee-koh-LIE REEM-skee–KOR-suh-kof

Camille Saint-Saens: kahm-EE sahn-SAHNS

Arnold Schoenberg: AR-nold SHOON-berg

Pyotr Ilyich Tchaikovsky:
PYAW-ter ihl-YICH chuh-KOFF-skee

gunwale

[GUN-ul]

the upper edge of the side of a ship or boat

The final member of the nautical aphonetic shibboleth words, *gunwale,* is yet another one demonstrating elision, in which certain letters aren't sounded out. In this case, there's no "wale" in gunwale. There is just a fading out "ul."

It is a portmanteau—a word formed by two other words or sounds that combines their meanings—from the Middle English *gonne-walle* (*gonne* meaning "gun," and *walle,* "wall") since it initially was exactly that—a metal strip that reinforced the ship to handle the weight of artillery—but now is simply the stiffened upper edge of the side of a ship or boat.

So why isn't it spelled "gunnel" if it isn't pronounced "gun-wale"? Well, *gunnel* actually is accepted as an alternative spelling and has been since the nineteenth century. (And more power to it, say we, since it looks like it sounds.) But as with those other maritime words, the illogical spelling remains more common and, to many eyes, appears more correct. That said, the saying "full to the gunnels" (or "packed to the gunnels"), meaning "extremely crowded," is more commonly seen spelled "gunnels" than "gunwales." If you Google the two phrases (and we did), "full to the gunnels" appears over one hundred thousand times more than "to the gunwales."

gyro

[YEE-roh]

sandwich made from meat that has been roasted on a rotating spit; served in a pita, usually with tomatoes, onions, and tzatziki (garlic yogurt sauce)

Gyro comes from the Greek *gyros* (circle or turning)—in this case, referring to succulent meat cooking on a slowly rotating spit. Most Americans pronounce *gyro* with an English soft *g* sound (as with *gyroscope,* which has the same word origin). But to the Greek guy slicing the roasted meat you just ordered off the spit, that sounds very, very wrong. The problem is that modern Greek doesn't have a *j* or *g* sound. The *g* is pronounced like a breathy *y* instead—"yee" (and the *y* with an *ee* sound).

If you want to sound supercorrect, add an *s*—as in *gyros*—which is the correct Greek singular. Just don't say *doner,* unless you're in a Turkish restaurant. *Doner* is the Turkish word for *gyros,* and according to Oxford food experts, the Turks actually established the modern cooking technique. The Greeks just later changed the word, and it stuck with American English since American Greeks are primarily responsible for mass-producing gyros. Today there are over fifty thousand gyro spits turning all over America . . . all pronounced "YEE-roh."

Halley's Comet

[HAL-eez comet]

a "short period" comet visible from Earth via the naked eye every seventy-five to seventy-six years

If you've been mispronouncing Halley's Comet, join the club. Only your friendly neighborhood astronomer probably noticed. For the record, Halley's comet, named after English astronomer Edmond Halley, is pronounced with a short *a* sound and rhymes with "Sally," not "daily."

According to one theory, the "HAY-lee" pronunciation came about after rock 'n' roller Bill Haley (pronounced, yes, "HAY-lee") and his Comets burst onto the musical scene. His name and his comets became confused with Sir Edmond and *his* comet, and the wrong pronunciation stuck.

But that's the romantic theory. The more prosaic reason is simply that "Haley" is a more common name than "Halley." (This jibes with another story about Bill Haley. Some say a friend of his noticed that many people were *already* mispronouncing Halley's comet as "HAY-lee's" and suggested that Bill take advantage of this and call his band the Comets.)

And now for one more wrinkle. According to the *New York Times*, there is contention about how Edmond Halley's name is actually pronounced. Everyone is sure it was not "HAY-lee," most say it's "HAL-ee" as in "alley," but still others say it's "HAW-lee." With all of this confusion, maybe we're better off with "HAY-leez" Comet after all.

haricot vert
(also haricot, haricot blanc, haricot bean)

[ARR-ee-coh vehr]

a thin green bean

With most French words that have been imported into English, the initial French pronunciation changes over time to become more anglicized. The word might still be spelled the French way, but we English speakers strip it of its original Gallic sound and substitute an anglicized approximation. This is *not* the case with *haricort vert*, which is why it can cause problems for non–French speakers and ends up on so many lists of most mispronounced food words.

When the word first appeared in English, it was often spelled a bit more phonetically—the *OED* lists *aricot beans* (1653), *arico* (1706), and *haricos* (1815). But over time, the spelling became standardized as *haricot*, particularly as French cuisine became popularized in the United States thanks to chefs like Julia Child—and the pronunciation remained the same.

Just as you trim the ends of a green bean for cooking, you should trim the *h* and the *t* in *haricot*. While you're at it, you also trim the *t* in *vert*. You can channel your inner Chef Jacques Pepin when you order these tasty beans in a restaurant. "I'd like the 'ARR-ee-coh vehr' s'il vous plait." (Okay, perhaps you should *also* trim the "s'il vous plait," unless you're in France.)

haute couture

[OAT kuh-TOOR]

*literally, "high fashion"; styles made by hand,
not mass produced, usually specifically for
individual clients; more loosely, fashions
made by top designers and/or fashion houses*

It's French, so you're forgiven if you, like so many others, botch this term by pronouncing the *h* (which, quelle horreur, the French don't do) and saying "hot," "hoat," or "hawt" and/or bollixing up *couture* as "coo-TOOR," "coo-CHOOR," or something like that.

You're also forgiven if you don't know that *haute couture* is a very specific type of fashion and a term protected by law in France. Designers or companies in France can only use *haute couture* to describe their fashions if they follow very specific rules (including creating made-to-order fashions for private clients, with one or more fittings; having an atelier [workshop] in Paris with at least fifteen full-time staff members; and creating a collection of at least fifty original designs to show to the public every January and July).

But just as the other French luxury item, champagne, has gotten bastardized a bit, so too has *haute couture*. Most nondesigners or French bureaucrats use it more loosely to apply to high-fashion clothing that might actually (gasp) be produced outside of Paris. But it's still properly pronounced the French way.

heartrending

[HART-ren-ding]

causing great distress, sorrow, mental pain,
or anguish; arousing deep sympathy

How many syllables do you see in this shibboleth word?
Three, right? Right; not four. Why then do so many
people persist in shoving an *er* in there and making it
"heart-rendering"? It's, well, heartrending.

To *rend* means to tear—so something that is heartrending
would be something that rips your heart, something that
is (to use similar terms) gut-wrenching or heartbreaking.
But *render* is an unrelated word with completely different
meanings, including to supply (as in services rendered), to
cause to be (rendered it possible), to depict (as in painting),
and, our personal favorite, to melt down (when used with
fat). None of these quite works with heart. . . . So *rend* it is.

These facts don't stop some people from insisting that
heart-rendering is a word that has a different meaning than
heartrending. It's enough to render one unconscious.

hegemony

[heh-JEM-uh-nee] (sometimes, particularly in the UK,
[heh-GEM-ah-nee], with a hard g)

*political, economic, or military leadership or dominance,
especially of one country or group over others*

This shibboleth word is one of those that many people
recognize in print but don't know how to pronounce. It's
not a word that often crops up in conversation unless you're
an academic or a political pundit. Based on our unscientific
survey (we asked friends), it is one of the words most
commonly mispronounced by "smart" people. Problem is,
it's also a word that crops up very often in "smart" articles
about world affairs and the like. As a result, some of those
smart people talk about "HEDGE-eh-moan-ee," which is
not the preferred pronunciation.

The funny thing is, enough people mispronounce it this
way that many people think it's wrong when pronounced
correctly. We stumbled upon a forum for linguaphiles and
the "how do you pronounce *hegemony*" thread was the
site of some heated debate—with many participants citing
professors or pundits they'd heard pronouncing *hegemony*
with the stress on the first syllable, and still others citing
dictionaries and other sources to back up their contention
that the second-syllable stress was correct. As with a number
of other shibboleth words, the nonpreferred pronunciation
has begun appearing in dictionaries as a second way to say
the word.

Hermione

[her-MY-oh-nee]

*name, chiefly British, and, in Greek mythology,
daughter of Helen and Menelaus and wife of Orestes.*

Hermione is best known to modern Muggles as the first
name of Hermione Granger of *Harry Potter* fame. So many
people were mispronouncing the name of this character
in the famous *Harry Potter* book series that the author,
J. K. Rowling, got sick of hearing "her-my-own," "her-my-
nee," "her-mee-oh-knee," and what some say was her
personal favorite, "hermy-one." So she had her character
Hermione give a pronunciation lesson to another character,
Victor Krum, in *Harry Potter and the Goblet of Fire*:
"Her-my-oh-nee," she tells him.

    Hermione was originally an ancient Greek name, the
feminine form of *Hermes*, the Greek messenger god. It came
into Latin as *Hermione* and from there to the English, who
have a certain and particular fondness for the name. There,
it had a surge of popularity in the early 2000s, but it has
since fallen off; it was and is a quite uncommon name in the
United States. Interestingly, in its native land of Greece,
the name now sounds quite different; for one thing, in
modern Greek, the *h* sound fell off, so, although there's
a port city with that name, it's now spelled and pronounced
"Ermioni."

homage

[HOM-idge] (and now, increasingly,
[AH-midge] or [o-MAHJ])

special honor or respect shown publicly

The mispronunciation of this word gives some people a great deal of grief, as evidenced by this angry letter to a show on National Public Radio: "The people you hear most frequently mispronouncing it as a French word are the Hollywood airheads in their commentary accompaniments on DVDs. 'o-MAHJ' . . . 'o-MAHJ' . . . 'o-MAHJ.' Give me a break!"

There are two issues here: the *h* and the "age" sound. Both arise from the Norman French origins of the word. When the Normans conquered England, they asked for "o-MAHJ" from their new subjects. They didn't pronounce the initial *h*, and they pronounced the "age" with a French soft *j* sound. But because *homage* was spelled with an *h* and English traditionally pronounces that *h*, so-called spelling pronunciation took over, changing it to a sounded *h* and the usual English pronunciation of "age," resulting in "HOM-idge."

However, more and more, people are saying "o-MAHJ" *à la francaise*. *Merriam-Webster* added it as an acceptable pronunciation, and probably more references will do so as time goes on. As the Normans conquered England, so, it seems, their pronunciation of *homage* is conquering English.

Houston Street (in New York City)

[HOUSE-ten street]

major east-west street in Manhattan, the dividing line between Greenwich Village and Soho

Ask a New Yorker how to get to Houston Street and, if you pronounce it like the city in Texas, you'll be pegged as an out-of-towner. (And definitely don't ask how to get to the corner of "Hewston Street" and the Avenue of the Americas . . . but that's another story.)

This isn't an example of New Yorkers being pains in the butt. The two Houstons are named after different people. The Texas city is named after Sam Houston (who pronounced it "HEWS-tun"), while Houston Street is named after William Houstoun (sometimes spelled "Houston," who always pronounced it "HOUSE-tun"). A delegate from Georgia for the Continental Congress, he was less than impressive to his fellow Georgia delegate William Pierce who wrote about him:

> As to his legal or political knowledge, he has very little to boast of. Nature seems to have done more for his corporeal than mental powers. His Person is striking, but his mind very little improved with useful or elegant knowledge.

So how did a rather meh Georgia pol wind up with a Manhattan street named after him? Simple: He married well—one Mary Bayard, whose father owned a large estate in Manhattan that included Houston Street—which made him a part of New York City lore.

I could care less

[eye cood care less]

to be completely uninterested in and utterly indifferent about the subject being referenced

This is one of those phrases that so many people missay—and one that consistently sets our teeth on edge because, of course, "I could care less" means the opposite:"I couldn't care less."

Some linguists claim that people omit the "n't" to make the phrase sarcastic. Linguist Steven Pinker wrote, "A good paraphrase is, 'Oh yeah, as if there was something in the world that I care less about.'" But most people—linguists and everyone else—think it's simply a sloppy bastardization of "I couldn't care less."

That said, it is so commonly used nowadays in the United States (other English speakers stick with the correct phrase) that it is becoming an idiom in its own right (or, well, wrong in this case!). It has been irritating people for years—Google News finds examples from the 1950s and the *OED* from 1966 on. So this is one shibboleth phrase we doubt will go away. That said, if you consistently "could care less," let's just say that most people will think you're a bit . . . careless.

iced tea

[ICED tee]

tea that is iced

You probably know it is spelled "iced tea," but you probably say "ice tea"—and you're not alone: In the United States, "ice tea" is now heard and seen more often than "iced tea."

"Iced" is technically correct because it is an adjective describing what was done to the tea—it was cooled by means of ice. This is why the original and "correct" term for ice cream was *iced* cream—cream that was iced. Because it was awkward to enunciate, the *d* and the *cr* in *ice cream* slid into each other (or assimilated) to make one sound. And now, the *d* and the *t* in *iced tea* are doing the same thing.

In both cases, the old "iced," which was an adjective, becomes a noun—"ice." *Ice tea* doesn't say what happened to the tea; now it's just two nouns describing what kind of tea it is. English is very good at creating these compound nouns. Watching *iced tea* change to *ice tea* is a linguistic education in itself. So next time you're sipping at your iced tea, think about it—you're sipping at language in action. But in the meantime, ask for *iced* tea.

ikat

[EE-kaht]

fabric dyeing technique in which yarns are tie-dyed before weaving; also the finished fabric itself

You see *ikat*—both a fabric and a dyeing technique—often in decor and fashion magazines, and it is just as often mispronounced. It is tempting when first confronted with this word to mentally pronounce it as if it were an Apple product, a robotic pet perhaps—"iCat," for example. But it's a Malay word, not a tech one, thus the not-as-straightforward-to-us "EE-kaht."

When used as a verb in Malay, *ikat* literally means to tie, bind, or fasten, so it is indeed descriptive of the technique. The end product, the dyed fabric, is also called *ikat*. Although the word is Malay and the fabric is often associated with Indonesia, the technique appears to have evolved independently in many different places. Dutch traders were the first to introduce ikats to Western culture. The *Oxford English Dictionary* has *ikat* being used in the English language first in 1931, in a book entitled *Ikat Technique and Dutch East Indian Ikats*. Since then this "on-loan word," as foreign words incorporated into English are sometimes called, has been more and more in evidence as the fabric boomed in popularity in the twenty-first century.

irregardless

[ri-GARD-lis]

in spite of circumstances, notwithstanding, anyway, despite everything

If you look up *irregardless* in the dictionary, you might not find it at all and if you do, it will probably say it's the nonstandard way of saying *regardless*. "Nonstandard" simply means that it is a regionalism or an informal word or phrase. In this case, we prefer to call *irregardless* not nonstandard, but nonright.

Irregardless is a colloquialism that probably grew from a mash-up (or, technically, a portmanteau) of the words *irrespective* and *regardless*. According to the *OED*, it was first used in South Carolina, although it was first mentioned in a dictionary (the *Wentworth American Dialect Dictionary*) in 1912 and said to be from western Indiana. It gained more widespread usage in the 1920s.

It is most common in speech. The 2015 Grammar Gripes Dictionary.com study found that 39 percent of Americans say they have heard *irregardless* used in place of *regardless*. It is not that common in print, though, and it is the subject of much debate—not so much in a "should you use it?" way (pretty much everyone agrees that you shouldn't), but in the "should it be considered a real word?" arena. Some lexicographers say, yes, it's a legitimate nonstandard word; others say it's not. The final strike against *irregardless* is that it is actually a double negative, since the prefix "ir-" means not and the suffix "-less" means without.

jibe

[jibe]

to be in agreement with, in harmony

This is mostly an Americanism, at least according to the august *OED*, which doesn't seem to quite approve. But it's an old Americanism—the 1860 edition of Bartlett's mentions Americans using it, and Mark Twain certainly did (although he spelled it with a *g*.) We're not talking about *gibe* (to taunt), or *jibing* (in sailing); we're talking about the common American use of *jibe* as in "to agree with," as in "The drop in jobless rates doesn't jibe with recent job gains."

The problem is that many people confuse *jibe* with *jive*, and put a *v* where a *b* should be. This changes the meaning entirely, not usually in a good way. Although *jive* can mean "fast jazz," it generally means "misleading" or "deceptive," as in "jive talking": telling people lies. So if you mispronounce *jibe* as *jive*, you're actually saying pretty close to the opposite of what you mean. And that's no jive.

HOW TO SOUND LIKE A PATRON OF THE ARTS

The Correct Way to Pronounce Ten of the More Difficult Visual Artists' Names

Diane Arbus: DEE-ahn AR-bus

Salvador Dalí: SAL-va-dor dah-LEE

Thomas Eakins: tom-us AY-kins

H. R. Giger: h r GHEE-gah

Giotto: JOT-oh

Käthe Kollwitz: KAY-tuh KOLL-vitz

Joan Miró: zhwan mi-ROH

Paul Klee: pawl klay

Claes Oldenburg: kloss OLD-en-berg

Wayne Thiebaud: wayne TEE-bow

kibosh

[KYE-bahsh]

put an end or stop to (almost exclusively used in the phrase "put a (or the) kibosh on" but sometimes used alone as a verb—as in "He kiboshed the plans")

For starters, it's pronounced "KYE-bahsh," not "KIH-bahsh" or "kye-BAHSH" or "kih-BAHSH." And it has been around a long time. You might think it emerged in the United States in the 1940s, since you can picture a tough guy in an old gangster movie talking about "putting the kibosh on that kind of talk." But it's actually much older. The *OED* has its first appearance in 1836 in Charles Dickens's *Sketches by Boz:* "[P]ut the kye-bosh [later editions had "kye-bosk"] on her, Mary."

No one is sure where the word came from. One theory is that it evolved from the Irish *caip bháis* (cap of death), referring to the black cap a judge put on when sentencing someone to death—which makes sense since, with typical confusing-to-us Irish spelling, *caip bháis* is pronounced "KYE-bosh" just like, yes, *kibosh*. Another theory is that it came from the Scots *kye* booties (cow boots put on cattle to keep them from straying). Others say it came from the Yiddish, and still others from the Hebrew *kbsh* or *khbsh*, or from the Turkish *boş* (pronounced "bosh").

The jury is out . . . so let's put the kibosh on further speculation.

Ku Klux Klan

[koo klux klan]

a semisecret racist society formed after the Civil War

The big-on-alliteration racist secret society isn't quite as alliterative as many people think. It's "KOO klux klan," not "KLOO klux klan." Supposedly, the *Ku* and *Klux* part of the Klan name came from the Greek word "kuklos"—or *circle*, used in this sense as a circle of like-minded people. The *Klan* is just alliteration.

The Klan was founded in the South after the Civil War by ex-Confederate soldiers who, for revenge, rode about at night in hoods terrorizing newly freed slaves. It faded out but after World War I it rose again, gaining over several million members who professed to be anti-Jewish, anti-Catholic, anti-immigrant, and later anti-Communist.

But the Klan was very pro the letter *K*, especially in combination with *l*. They added a host of ostensibly "kool" *kl* words to their lexicon: Klavern (local organization), Imperial Kleagle (recruiter), Klecktoken (initiation fee), Klonvocation (gathering), Kloreroe (delegate), Klaliff (vice president), Klokard (lecturer), Kludd and Imperial Kludd (chaplain), Kligrapp (secretary), Klabee (treasurer), Kladd ("conductor," in charge of initiating new members), Klarogo (inner guard, sergeant at arms), and Klexter (outer guard). (Yes, it sounds somewhat comical, even ridiculous—which is why it is difficult to believe that such an infantile yet hateful group could win any adherents.)

lackadaisical

[lack-uh-DAY-zi-cal]

*lacking enthusiasm; lazy in terms of
the amount of effort expended*

Lackadaisical is frequently mispronounced as "*lax*-adaisical"
by lackadaisical speakers. It's an easy mistake to make. It's so
tempting to elide or merge the *k* sound into the *a* sound and
create an *x* sound that shouldn't be there. Just try repeating
the word to yourself a few times, saying it faster and faster.
Also, the word *lax* fits in with the meaning of the word, so it
seems to some that *lackadaisical* is a strange sort of adjective
derived from *lax*.

It's not. *Lackadaisical* is an adjective that comes from
the Old English word *lackadaisy*, which comes, in turn,
from another word: *lack-a-day* or *alack the day*. All these
interjections were used, according to the *OED*, "to express
grief, concern, or regret at the events of a particular day."
You can suppose, then, that the adjective gradually assumed
the idea of a regrettable lack of effort in one's duties or
responsibilities in a given day. As Henry Fielding wrote in
1749 in his novel *Tom Jones*: "Good-lack-a-day! Why there
now, who would have thought it!"

liable

[LYE-uh-buhl]

legally responsible; likely to do or be something, usually in an undesirable sense

Liable is another word liable (we couldn't resist) to be mispronounced merely because we're lazy. It's easy to let your tongue slip and say "libel" instead of properly pronouncing all three syllables—"li-a-ble."

But if you mispronounce *liable* with two syllables—as *libel*—by getting rid of the *a*, you're now talking about slander and defamation, not legal responsibility or likelihoods. Big differences from one small syllable.

And now for one important note—*liable* usually refers to an undesirable or legal possibility, so don't use it for pleasant possibilities. Don't say "Our team is liable to win today!" unless, of course, you're betting on the other team. But you probably shouldn't bet against your own team anyway.

liqueur

[li-KERR]

alcoholic liquor, sweetened and flavored,
usually strong, typically served after dinner

This shibboleth word poses problems for those who want to sound sophisticated. Rather than the oh-so-declassé "li-KERR," they'll ask their server for a "li-KYOOR." Needless to say, all they've proven is that they're misinformed.

It's that "ueu" combo that gets 'em every time. It's a vowel string that doesn't often occur in English, but does in French . . . which is where *liqueur* came from in the eighteenth century from the French *liqueur*, liquor, or liquid. With the "ueu," it looks like it should be at the least an "oo" sound, if not a "yoo," as in "queue." But there's no "yoo" in French, where it's "LEE-kerr" (with that soft back-of-the-throat *r* that is so difficult for Americans).

The preferred pronunciation in the United States is the straightforward "li-KERR," similar to the French but with the stress on the second syllable. If you really can't stand the sound, you can get away with the British "li-KYIR"—which, while not the preferred, also appears as a pronunciation in American dictionaries. But "li-KYOOR" is only an affectation, something that will drive most educated people to, well, drink. So don't ask for a "li-KYOOR" (and never ask for a "per-NOD" either . . .).

long-lived

[long-LIEvd] or [long-LIVVED]

having a long life or existence; lasting a long time

This is a no-brainer, right? Well . . . no. The issue at hand is the pesky homophone *lived*. By itself, it can be correctly pronounced two different ways—with a short or a long *i*. So which is right in this case? And—drumroll—the long-*i*-form "LIEved" has it! Kind of. . . .

The reason is found in the long, long life history of this word. Back in medieval times when Middle English was spoken, this word was spelled "long-lifed" and was pronounced with three distinct syllables—long LIEV-ed. Yes, that *ed* ending was always pronounced (pronounce-ed!) separately. You will note that in spite of the spelling it wasn't pronounced "long LIFF-ed." This is because the *f* wasn't our *f* but more a blurring of *f* and *v* . . . which is how the spelling of the word slowly drifted into the current spelling ("lived") to match the pronunciation. But since "live" can be pronounced either LIEV or LIVV, the second pronunciation also became commonly used. Thus we wind up back at the beginning of this long-lived issue.

Louisville

[LOO-uh-vull], [LOO-ih-vull]

largest city in Kentucky

Old joke: Quick—How do you pronounce the capital of Kentucky? Lewisville or Looeyville? Answer: Frankfort.

Our father told us this joke when we were young, and we thought it was hilarious. We've grown older and now we know there is another wrinkle to the joke. "Louisville" isn't pronounced either way. According to natives of this large city, it's "LOO-uh-vull" or "LOO-ih-vull."

It was named after King Louis XVI of France, and the pronunciation of the city name today is a modified version of the French pronunciation—although the French way of saying it sounds more like "LOO-eh-veeye."

Such are the ways of language and pronunciation. Not-so-far-away St. Louis is not pronounced with any modicum of French pronunciation at all. It's pronounced "Saint Lewis," the completely American way. And meanwhile, back in Kentucky itself, just to be difficult, there's another town, the charming small town of Versailles, pronounced . . . "Ver-SALES." A Frenchman would probably wince, but when in Les États-Unis. . . .

machination

[mack-uh-NAY-shun]

plotting and intrigue

In the *American Journal of Education* (Volume 17, 1867), there is a report on a certain notorious "Miss — from the New Jersey Normal School" who taught her class to pronounce *machination* as "mash-in-nation." "There can be no possible excuse for such carelessness, or rather ignorance," thundered the old journal—and while we agree that *machination* is best said with a hard *k* sound, Miss — had ample excuse for her pronunciation.

Machination comes from an old Latin word with the same spelling, meaning "machine-making." As we've mentioned before, the Romans pronounced their *ch* as *k*, and the Italian speakers followed suit (as in "Machiavelli"). But words migrate and pronunciations change. Many Latin words with *ch* changed when they became English, especially when they were imported via the French, like *machine*, which no one pronounces "mak-EEN." But oddly, *machination* didn't make that switch even though it contains the word *machine* within it, which poses this question: If English speakers don't now pronounce machine with a Latin *k* sound, why should they pronounce *machination* with one? We agree with that reasoning on a logical basis, but language is hardly logical. So for now, especially for those who wish to sound well educated, stick with the old hard *k* pronunciation.

Magdalen (also Magdalene)

[MAWD-lin]

(1) one of the great colleges of Oxford (Magdalen) with graduates that include playwright Oscar Wilde and physicist Erwin Schrodinger; (2) a major college of Cambridge (Magdalene) with graduates that include C. S. Lewis and John McPhee

St. Mary Magdalen(e)—the reformed ex-prostitute who washed Jesus's feet and was present at the Crucifixion—gave her name to two major colleges in England: Magdalen College at Oxford University and Magdalene College at Cambridge University, both pronounced not "MAG-da-lin" but . . . "MAWD-lin." What happened?

It's likely that the *g* was lost because, as with so many words and names in English, the prestigious French pronunciation (with a British twist) was preferred. (Her name in modern French is *Madeleine*). Mary Magdalene also graced the English language with a noun, *maudlin*, spelled as it is pronounced, which means "sentimental."

But don't go assuming all English Magdalens are maudlins. Magdalens that are not connected to the colleges, such as St. Mary Magdalen Church and Magdalen Street, are pronounced with three syllables and the *g*. When in doubt, you can do what Oxford students used to do (and maybe do still)—call Magdalen "Maggers."

marquis

[MAR-kwiss]

English aristocratic title below a duke and above an earl

No, that's not a typo in the pronunciation section. If you're talking about a British holder of the title "marquis," it is "MAR-kwiss" with an *s*. If you're talking about a French holder of the title, it's "mar-KEE," as in the Marquis de Lafayette.

It gets a bit more complicated. Actually the more proper and correct English word for an English marquis is *Marquess* (MAR-kwess) with an *e*, but also pronounced with an *s*. But, particularly in recent years, the French spelling has migrated across the Channel, possibly because *Marquess* sounds like a feminine title and visions of an English lord in drag drift into mind. (The womanly equivalent for *Marquess* is the intimidating-looking *Marchioness*—pronounced "MAHR-shuh-nis."

All you have to know is that when in England, do as the English do and pronounce the *s*, or be really correct and say "MAR-kwess"—and be thankful that there are many more easily pronounced barons, dukes, and earls.

mascarpone

[mas-car-POH-neh] or [mas-car-POH-nay]

mild Italian soft cheese made from cow's milk

Let's start with the three basics about mascarpone:
(1) There is no *r* in the first syllable. (2) It has four syllables.
(3) Did we mention there is no *r* in the first syllable?

This is one of the most commonly mispronounced
food words. All too often, people who should know better,
including chefs, food critics, and Italian Americans, say
"MARS-capone" (much like Al Capone but with a "mars"
instead).

The word and the cheese both come from the Lombardy
region of Italy. No one is absolutely sure of its origins, but
one possibility is that it derived from *mascarpa* or *mascarpia*,
a type of local ricotta cheese. This makes sense because both
cheeses are made in similar ways. There's another more far-
fetched but interesting origin story put forth by two Italian
etymologists in the 1970s. They theorize that it evolved
from the classical Latin *mascarpiō*—a word used by ribald
Roman author Petronius that some scholars think alluded
to masturbation—and point out that in southern Italy, the
phrase "far ricotta" (which literally means "to make ricotta")
is a slang way of saying "to masturbate." This theory is by no
means widely accepted (and, admittedly, a bit too evocative
to think about when eating the tasty cheese . . .).

mauve

[mohv]

pale purple color between lilac and violet

No, you don't pronounce this color as if you're making a kiss sound and adding a *v*—"mwahve." It's simply "mohv." Okay, perhaps it's not quite that simple since some dictionaries say it can also be the more American "mawve." *Merriam-Webster* even has that as its preferred pronunciation, with "mowve" as the second pronunciation. But this Americanized pronunciation is usually met with sneers, as in an entry in the online *Urban Dictionary*, which succinctly said, "Only idiots pronounce the color 'mauve' 'mawv.'"

As a French import (it comes from the French *mauve* [mallow], a plant that has pale purple flowers), *mauve* raises the usual pronunciation problem. Should the word retain some of its "Frenchness" or has the American sound become pervasive enough that it reigns supreme? In French, there's a soupçon ("soop-SAWHn," if you were curious) of a second syllable—"mowva"—that trails off. But it's most definitely "mow," not "maw." But in the United States, you technically can get away with either pronunciation, even though "mohv" seems more accepted. (And of course, you could always just say "light purple" and be done with it.)

mischievous

[MIS-chuh-vus]

wanting to or causing trouble, most often in a playful way

We almost didn't include this word in our shibboleth collection because, although it often appears on lists of mispronounced words, we thought it was left over from the past. But once we really started listening, we discovered that many people still say it incorrectly—among them a few friends, several television hosts, two anchorpeople, and five politicians. *Merriam-Webster* helpfully adds that former president Herbert Hoover was guilty as well. They all fell prey to the "let's add an *i* in there and make it four syllables" syndrome, making the word "mis-CHEE-vee-us."

To make things worse, this mispronunciation also lends itself to spelling errors. When people add the extra syllable, they often also add that *i* when they spell it, writing it "mischievious." This mistake goes back many years, as far back as the sixteenth century, even though the word was initially spelled somewhat phonetically as the mid-fourteenth-century Anglo-Norman word *meschevous*. Probably the mispronunciation and spelling then and now arises because it and *grievous* are the only two words in English that end in "vous," while a greater number end in "vious" (*devious, envious, previous*, etc.). So one might say that it would be "GREE-vee-us" to say "mis-CHEE-vee-us."

misled

[miss-LED]

led astray, deceived; past tense of mislead

A confession: When younger, one of us pronounced this word as "myselled," in other words, as the past tense of a (completely imaginary) verb, *to misle*. According to several surveys, this is a surprisingly common mistake. Even the august *Chronicle of Higher Education*, with its target audience of university educators, mentions it and explains how *misled* has, well, misled so many of us.

In short, *misled* is formed from the prefix "mis-" (meaning "in a wrong way") and the past tense of the verb "to lead." The problem is that "to lead" is an irregular verb—it forms its tenses in its own merry way. So while there's mislead, misleads, and misleading, if it happened in the past it's mis*led*. So that's a problem. This past tense spelling tempts us to think it's the past tense of another verb, *to misle*—as in "She misles me." But, of course, there's no such verb as *misle* in any form. So don't be misled!

Möbius (also Moebius)

[MEUH(r)-bee-uhs]

August Ferdinand Möbius (1790–1868), German
mathematician who described the famous Möbius strip
as a surface having only one side and one edge

Years ago on a *Jeopardy* show, the leading contestant gave the question to the answer in the Mathematics category: "Who was MERR-bius?" (with a pronunciation heavy on the "err"). Host Alex Trebek said, no, the correct question was "Who was MOE-bius?" A few minutes later, after some discussion offstage, he announced that the contestant's question was correct after all.

The issue, of course, is how to pronounce German. Mathematician Möbius spelled his name with an umlaut (two dots) over the *o*, giving it the distinctly German pronunciation in between *er* and *o*. Short of getting a German to pronounce it for you, purse your lips and say "Meu-" and then add "bee-uhs" (as in "dubious"), and you've got it. There is a slight *r* sound to the name, but not as exaggerated as what was heard on *Jeopardy*.

It's a shame that Möbius gave his name to his famous Möbius strip instead of another German mathematician with the easily pronounceable name of J. B. Listing, who also independently discovered it at about the same time. His name was given not to the strip but to a type of number called a Listing number. And unfortunately, Listing numbers do not come into common discourse as frequently.

HOW TO SOUND PHILOSOPHICAL

Pronouncing the Names of Fifteen of the Great Minds

Karl Barth: karl bart

Walter Benjamin: WAHL-ter BEN-yameen

George Berkley: jorge BARK-lee

Mihaly Csikszentmihalyi: me-HY CHEEK-sent-me-high

W. E. B. DuBois: w e b duh-BOYZ

Michel Foucalt: mee-SHELL foo-COH

Philip Gourevitch: fil-ip guh-RAY-vitch

John Maynard Keynes: jahn MAY-nard kayns

Plotinus: ploh-TYNE-us

W. G. Sebald: w g ZAY-bald

Henry David Thoreau: HEN-ree DAY-vid THOR-oh

Max Weber: max VAY-ber

Simone Weil: zee-MOHN vay

Ludwig Wittgenstein: LOOD-vig vit-gehn-SHTAYN
or vit-gehn-SHTINE

Slavoj Žižek: SLAH-voy ZHEE-zhek

Moët et Chandon

[Mwett eh SHA(n)-doh]

famous French champagne

If you want to sound like a true sophisticate, pronounce the final *t* in Moët. Many people don't, thinking they're sounding more French that way. But Moët should sound more Dutch than French.

The founder of this famous French champagne company, official supplier to Queen Elizabeth among others around the world, had a Dutch name, not a French one, so he pronounced his name the Dutch way with a sounded *t* at the end. It's "Mwett" (either alone or in combination with *et Chandon*), not "Moay." That's how the French say it, how it's pronounced in top New York restaurants, and (probably) how Queen Elizabeth pronounces it as well. And, of course, don't pronounce the *t* in *et*.

Pronouncing *Moët* correctly can actually lead to problems, according to Helen Vause, public relations spokesperson for Moët et Chandon in New Zealand. "When I say it the right way, people often look slightly embarrassed and think, "She doesn't know how to pronounce it, poor dear." Maybe she should order Veuve Clicquot, the great rivals to Moët, instead, being careful to *not* pronounce the *t* in *Clicquot*.

moussaka

[moo-sah-KAH]

dish of ground meat (such as lamb or beef) and layered sliced vegetables, often eggplant, with béchamel sauce

Even the *Oxford English Dictionary* gets this wrong—it's not the commonly said "moo-SAH-kah," nor is it "MOO-sah-kah." The preferred foodie and Greek restaurant pronunciation of this famous dish has the accent on the last syllable, just like the Greek word for this dish, *moussakas*. (But in English, we just leave off the last *s*.)

So when in Greek restaurants, do as the Greeks do, order "moo-sah-KAH." But maybe you shouldn't tell your Greek waiter what the *Oxford English Dictionary* says about this dish so beloved in Greece—that the word actually came to Greece via their once archenemies, the Turks, from the Arabic word *musaqqā*, "that which is fed liquid," referring perhaps to the béchamel sauce. Just stick with the correct accent and you'll be fine.

Nguyen

[wen]

Vietnamese surname

Almost everyone who doesn't speak Vietnamese mispronounces this very common Vietnamese name. A young man named, of course, Nguyen, recently put up a blog post of some of the mispronunciations he's heard of his name—Nigwenn, Noogin, Nigguhwin, Newjwin—and then another Nguyen added Nuh-goo-in.

It's a name that shouldn't be mispronounced since you'll probably come across it many times. It's the fifty-seventh most common surname in the United States, and estimates are that 40 percent of all Vietnamese have this name. (Note: We're using the term "surname" because the Vietnamese like the Chinese traditionally put their "last" name first, as in Smith John, not John Smith, although many reverse this in Western countries). In Australia, "Nguyen" is second only to "Smith" in the Melbourne phone book.

For the record, it's pronounced something like "wen." The Vietnamese have a slight, very soft *g* sound in front, but "wen" is close enough. Since Vietnamese is a tonal language, a better way to pronounce it is to divide the wen into two syllables, and say "wen" as if asking the question "When?" with the "whe" in a falling tone, and the "en" in a rising tone, as in intoning "uh-huh." You could say that nguyen you've done that, you'll have it!

niche

[neesh] *or* [nitch]

shallow recess in wall for a sculpture or other decorative object; a place or position suitable or appropriate for a person or thing; a market segment

Here's yet another French-derived shibboleth word with that pesky "che" ending that often throws people. In this case, instead of (wrongly) going for a super-faux-French sound and saying "ni-chay," many people super-anglicize it and say "nitch." This had been wrong until recently, as the preferred pronunciation was the one used since the seventeenth century—a soft, long *e* "neesh" like the fourteenth-century French word meaning recess for a dog, or kennel.

But as "nitch" has become a more commonly used pronunciation, it also has become more widely accepted. It's even become the preferred pronunciation in some dictionaries. It can get quite confusing if you're a stickler for proper pronunciation. This is why *niche* wound up on *Merriam-Webster's* word-of-the-year list in 2013 as more and more people looked it up to be sure they were saying it right.

nip it in the bud

[nip it in thuh buhd]

to stop something from happening before it has a chance to develop into something larger

This shibboleth phrase falls prey to the "trouble with soundalikes" effect—in this case, switching "bud" to its quasi homophone "butt." In linguistics, these almost-soundalikes are called *minimal pairs*. But in this case, let's just call it wrong.

And "bud" is unequivocally correct. The phrase refers to a spring frost killing flower buds so they will never bloom. Speaking of bloom, the phrase actually was first "nip it in the bloom"—and appeared in a 1595 romance by Henry Chettle. Only a few years later, in 1606 or 1607, a comedy *Woman Hater* had the line "Yet I can frowne and nip a passion Euen in the bud." And so "bud" took root.

But then "butt" blundered onto the scene and the rest is linguistic history. The, um, bottom line? Be sure to say "nip it in the *bud*" or it can come back and bite you in the . . . oh, never mind.

nuptial

[NUHP-shuhl]

a wedding; of or pertaining to a wedding

Nuptial is one of those shibboleth words that lands people into trouble because of how it looks and how it *ought* to sound. In this case, it looks like it should have three syllables. But in spite of the spelling, it's two syllables, not three. It's not "nup-shi-al" or "nup-shu-al." It's plain old "NUHP-shuhl." It comes from the French *nuptial*, which is from the Latin *nuptialis*. In its first printed appearance in English in a 1490 translation of *Eneydos*, it was spelled as the somewhat odd-looking but phonetically sound "nupcyalle."

Why is there a temptation to mispronounce the word? It's probably simply that it sounds better to our ears for euphonic reasons. At least we're not talking about the original word for *wedding*—from the great-granddaddy of English (and most other languages in Europe and the Indian subcontinent), Proto-Indo-European. The verb "to marry" or "to wed" was *sneubh*. So would *nuptial* have sounded something vaguely like "sneubhialis"? Maybe we're better off with *nuptial*, mispronunciation problems and all.

Oaxaca

[wa-HA-ka]

a Mexican state

Oaxaca is a large state of Mexico on the Pacific Coast with what looks like a tongue twister of a name: O-ax-a-ca. But if you know what you're doing, it's really not that tough.

Its name in English (and Spanish) is based on the name the Nahuatl people (known also as the more easily pronounced Aztecs) called the valley where they lived. They named it Huaxyacac after a wooded prominence in the valley covered with acacia trees called *huāx-in* (also known as *guaje*) trees.

This sounded something like "wa-sha-cac," which the Spanish conquerors of Mexico apparently had problems pronouncing, particularly with that final *c*. They chose to drop the *c* and wound up spelling it "Oaxaca"—with the *oa* substituting for the *hua* sound. At the time, the *x* was pronounced *sh*. As times changed, so did Spanish pronunciation. That *x* sound became a harsh *h* sound; and so we have "wa-HA-ka" today.

oeuvre

[OO-vruh]

body of work produced by an artist, composer, or writer

Oeuvre is one of those words that can cause strong individuals to panic, or at least give them pause. It is clearly French with that frightening gauntlet of three vowels in a row followed by an *re* ending. Is it "OH-vray," "oh-EE-ewe-ver," "OH-ewe-vera"? "Aha," one might think logically, "it's in 'hors d'oeuvre,' so it must be pronounced the same."

But *oeuvre* isn't pronounced "erve." It's "OO-vruh" in the United States, with a stress on the first syllable and a strong *oo* sound, and "uh-vruh" in the UK, without the same initial punch or *oo* sound. The word comes from the French *oeuvre* (work). Of course, in the French, it's pronounced differently—with that sort of rolled *r* that dies out at the end. But as with many French imports, the American pronunciation is a modified version, so we don't have to try to approximate that typical Gallic sound. Our pronunciation is much easier, the dummy's guide to *ouevre* pronunciation. Just don't, when asking for hors d'oeuvres, ask for "or-DOO-vruh."

ombré

[AHM-bray]

shaded, more specifically, the gradual blending of the shades of one color, usually going from light to dark

Ombré is one of those fashion terms that looks so easy to say but that is often mispronounced because of the different possibilities that "bré" ending suggest: "ber," "brr," "bray"? The temptation often is to opt for the "ahmber" pronunciation. But think of a bit actor in an old Western talking about that bad hombre who has been terrorizing the border town and you've got it.

It was first used to describe fabrics back in the early 1800s, when a specific printing block was used to print a light to dark shading of the same color on fabric. Later, machines produced ombré fabrics by using thread dyed in the different shades of a color. Since then, the concept of ombré tones has moved beyond fabrics to hair coloring, home decor, cake decoration, and more.

The word, like so many other fashion terms, comes from French—in this case, the word *ombrer* (to shade), which came from the Italian *ombrare*, which came from the Latin *umbrare* which came from the noun *umbra*, shade. It's a nice straightforward evolution, much like the small gradations in color and hue that the word describes.

ophthalmologist

[off-tha(l)-MOLL-uh-jist]

*medical doctor who specializes in the treatment
of eye problems and diseases*

Why is *ophthalmologist* on so many "most mispronounced
words" lists? we wondered. It's a long word, yes, but not
a complicated one. We have been saying it for years, since
we both have been seeing eye doctors since we were
kids. But then we learned that there *is* a common way to
mispronounce it . . . and, of course, we have been doing it
all of our lives.

First there's the *ph*—which we and many others turn
into a *p*—giving us "OP" as in *optics*. But it's "oph," from
the Greek *ophthalmos* (the eye), not, as with optics, directly
from the Greek adjective *optikios*—of or relating to sight.
So it is an *f* sound just like *phone*. Then there's the sneakier
problem. Look closely at the word. There are two *l*'s in there,
aren't there? Why, then, do 99.9 percent of English speakers
drop the first one? (Okay, we lied about the 99.9 percent.
Let's just say many, many people don't see that first *l*. Maybe
they need an ophthalmologist. And now that we've gotten
that off our chest. . . .)

orangutan

[aw-RANG-uh-tan] (also uh-RANG-uh-tan)

*large reddish anthropoid ape from the
jungles of Borneo and Sumatra*

If you're like most people, you're probably wondering what
happened to the *g* at the end of the word. It was never there.
There's no such thing as an "orangutang" even though large
numbers of people think there is.

The word comes from Malay (actually, pidgin Malay,
spoken among people from different linguistic backgrounds
in the bustling multicultural markets of Southeast Asia).
"Orang" (with a hard *g* ending) means "man"; and "utan"
means "forest." Combine them and you've got that funny
looking, long-armed, gentle, friendly, and now sadly
endangered jungle ape of Indonesia and Malaysia.

Fortunately for those of us who keep on pronouncing
orangutan with a final *g* (and count one of us among the
very guilty), at least one dictionary, the always-quick-to-
add-new-pronunciations (as you may already have noted)
Merriam-Webster, seems to have reluctantly given up and
now considers both pronunciations to be correct. But
if you're ever in Malaysia on vacation, by all means cut
out that offending *g*. A recent article in Malaysian media
stated that Malaysians "cringe every time [they] hear
[people] mispronounce 'orangutan'" but added that they're
too polite to correct them.

Oregon

[OR-i-guhn]

*U.S. state on the Pacific coast,
between California and Washington*

Let's cut to the chase: there's no "gone" or "gon" (as in polygon) in Oregon, even though most non-West Coast Americans pronounce it that way. Rather, there's a "gun"— a short "gun" that you say a little faster than you'd normally say it, and it ends up sounding almost like "gin."

No one is sure about the origin of the name *Oregon*, so no one knows why it's pronounced as it is. But for many Oregonians, pronouncing their state name correctly is very important. As a polite reminder, the University of Oregon bookstore (and numerous other places) sell sweatshirts, socks, and bumper stickers that spell out "Oregon" phonetically as "O-R-Y-G-U-N" (with a short *y* or *e* sound in "gun," of course). This was the brainchild of Harold (Hal) Evenson, a 1968 University of Oregon graduate who created Orygun decals because his Air Force buddies couldn't pronounce *Oregon* correctly. He's still got a lot of work ahead of him, so we're doing our part here too.

Pago Pago

[PAHNG-o PAHNG-o]

*major city and de facto capital of
American Samoa, in the South Pacific*

Many people have heard of or read about Pago Pago. It's the quintessential South Seas tropical paradise and a favorite tourist destination made famous by novelist Somerset Maugham in his books. If it's so famous, you'd think at least we could keep the pronunciation straight. But it's written "Pago Pago" and pronounced "pango pango." No one is certain why, but the spelling confusion probably began when Christian missionaries visited the island. They brought along printing presses and movable type with them to help print Bibles and Christian literature in the local language of Samoan, and here ran into a problem.

Samoan is an *n*-heavy language—a nasal-sounding *n* follows *every a*—so naturally, with so many *n*'s required, the missionaries quickly ran out of *n*'s in their type boxes. So they skipped them for the most part, and everyone just assumed that a nasal *n* sound followed every *a*, even if it wasn't printed. Interestingly, in nearby Tonga (a mere five hundred miles away by ship), the locals for years spelled their island "Toga" but pronounced it "tonga." They officially added the *n* to the spelling of their island in 1950 while the Samoans have kept their *n* off.

papier-mâché

[PAY-per-muh-SHAY]

*a mixture of paper and glue or paper, flour,
and water that becomes hard when it dries;
used for crafts and decorations*

There are people who see the French spelling of papier-mâché and think surely it should be pronounced in a French-ish way. And so we hear of something made of "pah-pee-AY muh-shay." To which we can only say, "non, non, non."

Even though it comes (obviously) from the French—*papier* (paper) and *mâché* (the past participle of "to chew"), the pronunciation has been anglicized. So it is pronounced as plain old "paper," not "pah-pee-ay" or "pah-pee-er" or anything else that attempts to sound French. In fact, it's sometimes spelled "paper-mache" and has been since the later 1700s.

There was a *Seinfeld* episode in which George got irritated with his girlfriend because she kept calling papier-mâché "pah-pee-YAY MAH-shay," and we agree that Americans should steer clear of that pretension. Some people get a pass though—for example, David Bowie refers to "pah-pee-ya mash-ay" in his 1974 song "Candidate." This is allowed because he was British, and the British pronunciation is "pah-pee-ya-MAH-shay."

pathos

[PAY-thuhs] (or [PAY-thoss]—rhyming with *toss*)

quality or trait that evokes sorrow, pity, or sympathy

In spite of appearances or impulse, in English there is no "path" in *pathos* and there's no "o" either. So it isn't "PATH-oss," "PAY-thoes," nor any other combo of these sounds. And it is pathetic to pronounce it otherwise.

Actually, the word *pathetic* is possibly why people think it's "PATH-os"; it is a more common word and seems like the logical pronunciation. But even though *pathetic* has the "ath" sound, *pathos* doesn't. What makes it more confusing is that *pathos* comes from the Greek word *pathos*—which is pronounced "PATH-os." Why did it change in English to "PAY-thuhs"? We couldn't find any definitive reason for this (and we certainly tried) so are forced to presume that as with so many other words, it just changed over time. And there was a lot of time for this to happen since it first appeared in written English in 1591 in the second edition of Edmund Spenser's *The shepheardes calender*. (The first edition had *pathos* written in Greek.)

Because the information on *pathos* is so thin, we're throwing in an extra-credit shibboleth word: the infrequently used look-alike to *pathos*, *bathos* (an anticlimax), is pronounced "BAY-thoss," not "BATH-oss."

HOW TO SOUND LIKE A CAPTAIN OF INDUSTRY

The Eleven Most Commonly Mispronounced Brand and Corporate Names

Fage (Greek yogurt sold in the United States): FAH-yay

Gieves and Hawkes (famous Savile Row tailors): geevs and hawx (with a hard *g*)

Huawei (giant Chinese phone manufacturer that recently considered changing its name to make it easier for American and European customers to pronounce): wah-wey

Hoegaarden (classic white Belgian beer): HOO-gar-duhn

Laphroiag (single malt scotch): la-FROYG

Miele (high-end home-appliance manufacturer): MEEL-uh

Porsche (German sports car): POR-shuh

Renault (French car): REN-oh

Saucony (running shoe): SOCK-a-knee

Stolichnaya (Russian vodka): stoh-LEECH-nye-a

Zagat (review guide publisher): za-GAT

Pepys (Samuel)

[peeps]

famous seventeenth-century English naval official, known for his intimate and evocative diary

Samuel Pepys gave the world his famous diary, filled with insights into life in seventeenth-century England—and with titillating details of a quite vigorous love life, including liaisons with at least three women named Betty. Pepys also gave the world the baffling pronunciation of his name, one of the most mispronounced famous names in English. Many scholars and literature lovers share an embarrassing secret: they once mispronounced it as (horrors!) "peppis."

Interestingly, other branches of the Pepys family pronounced it just like that. In his *Genealogy of the Pepys Family* (1887), Walter Pepys gives three main pronunciations used by different branches of the family—"peps," "peeps," and "peppis" (along with seventeen different spellings) and says that "peppis" is the probable original "correct" pronunciation since the name originally came from the French, *Pepy*. (Others dispute this purported origin.)

According to Pepys scholar Henry Wheatley, the Pepys of the Samuel Pepys branch was probably originally pronounced "peps" or "papes," and spelled "peaps" or more commonly, "peyps." Along the way, as English sounds changed, the short *e* became a long *ee* sound, and the *y* and the *p*, for unknown reasons, were transposed. So we now have *Pepys*, which is pronounced like the brightly hued soft chick candy: Peeps.

peremptory

[puh-REMP-tuh-ree]

*demanding obedience or immediate attention,
especially when referring to a person's
manner of actions; imperious*

Peremptory falls into the category of tempting-transposition shibboleth words: words that fall prey to metathesis. These are those words that entice you to transpose two letters, forming a new word that sounds right but is wrong.

In this case, it's the "per" that is problematic. It is easy to switch the letters around to get the ever-so-common "pre" prefix and pronounce the word "pree-EMP-tor-ee." It's especially easy because it includes the real word *preempt* . . . so it sounds kosher. But, needless to say, there is no such word as "preemptory." If you want to use the adjectival form of *preempt*, you would say "preemptive."

Peremptory has always led with a "per." It evolved from the Latin *peremptorius*, from *perimere* (to destroy; also, later, to take away entirely) to become a legal term in late Middle English. So obey the laws of pronunciation and use a "per" rather than a "pre."

phô

[fuh]

*Vietnamese noodles, served in a beef
(or sometimes chicken) broth*

Here's a well-known foodie joke to remind you how to
pronounce these wonderful Vietnamese noodles: Q: What do
you call a line in a Vietnamese noodle shop? A: Phô Queue.

Groan. But yes, it's pronounced "fuh"—a slightly rolling
uh sound, as in *fur* without the *r* or almost exactly like the
French word for fire, *feu*. And sure enough, the French *feu*
is usually considered to be the origin of the word. Many
linguists trace the beginnings of *phô* back to Hanoi of the
1860s under French colonial rule, and perhaps to *pot-au-feu*
(pot on the fire)—the name for a classic Burgundian beef
stew made with vegetables.

Before then, the Vietnamese rarely ate beef, but with the
French, it became a major food item (although phô can also
be made with chicken, called *phô ga*). The Vietnamese added
noodles to the "pot" and then chopped off the "pot-au" from
the classic French dish's name, and thus, a new all-Vietnamese
classic was created. But others (particularly in China) trace
phô's origins to the beef-eating Chinese, with a Chinese
word for noodles, *fen*, transmogrifying to *fuh* in Vietnamese.
Whatever the origins, at least everyone agrees on one thing:
it's not pronounced "fo."

piquant

[PEE-kent]

*in food, having a pleasant, sharp taste; more generally,
pleasantly stimulating or exciting*

It's not "PEE-kwant" nor is it "pee-KHANT." The preferred
pronunciation stresses the "PEE" and has the "quant"
pronounced as "kent." ("Kahnt" is also acceptable, but
not preferred.) It comes from the fourteenth-century Middle
French *piquant*, which as a noun initially meant "something
thrown," and as an adjective meant "having a sharp taste."

There's a long history of *piquant* being pronounced
incorrectly. The 1889 book *Seven Thousand Words Often
Mispronounced: A Complete Hand-Book of Difficulties in
English Pronunciation, Including an Unusually Large Number
of Proper Names and Words and Phrases from Foreign
Languages* by the euphoniously named William Henry
Pinkney Phyfe pronounces it with more Gallic flair—with
the "quant" rhyming with the French *vin*. In 1917, Frank
H. Vizetelly came out with an even more ambitious work:
*A Desk-Book of Twenty-Five Thousand Words Frequently
Mispronounced: Embracing English Words, Foreign Terms,
Bible Names, Personal Names, Geographical Names, and
Proper Names of All Kinds Current in Literature, Science,
and the Arts, That Are of Difficult Pronunciation, Carefully
Pronounced, Annotated, and Concisely Defined and Indicating
the Preferences of the Leading Dictionaries from 1732 to 1924.*
Mr. Vizetelly is clear: "PEE-kent" is preferred. And if it's good
enough for Mr. Vizetelly, it's good enough for us.

pique

[peek]

*verb: stimulate, intrigue; noun: irritation or resentment
(usually with "fit of" as in a "fit of pique")*

This is a shibboleth word in two ways. There's the pronunciation issue: it is "peek," with the "que" as a simple *k* sound since the word came from the French *piquer*, meaning "to irritate or prick." And there's the spelling issue: many people who know how to say the word in conversation spell it as it sounds—"peak"—especially with the phrase "pique my interest."

It's an example of homophonic homonymic horror— when a word sounds just like another word, but is spelled differently, as in "My interest was piqued when I peeked at the peak." The Google Ngram Viewer (which charts usage in books) shows that "piqued my interest" is most common, but "peaked my interest" began surging in 1980 and keeps going up.

It shouldn't be too surprising, though. From the beginning, "pique" was spelled numerous ways. Among them, from the 1500s to the 1700s, "pyke," "picke," "peake," and "peek." But *pique* as it is currently spelled became the norm from the mid-1700s on.

Note: If it has an accent over the *e*, it is a noun referring to a type of fabric and is pronounced "pee-KAY." However, beware! Sometimes the fabric is spelled without the accent, and is still said "pee-KAY," so pay attention to the context.

plethora

[PLETH-er-uh]

too many; a large or excessive amount

Poor *plethora*! For one thing, a plethora of people insist on pronouncing it "ple-THOR-a," which is almost okay if they're trying to imitate the ancient Greeks from whom the word originated. The Greeks had a long *e* sound as well as a long *o* sound in the word. It came from their word *pletho* (I fill). But from the Greeks it went to the Romans and then to the English, and along the way, the *e* and the *o* became shorter, and it came to be pronounced "PLETH-er-uh" and accented on the first syllable.

Along came a new meaning for the word. It came to mean not "full," but "*too* full." Doctors in the 1500s used *plethora* in the sense of an excess of bodily fluids, a very bad thing according to the medical theories of the day. And from there it came to mean "too much in general," or "too many," in the modern sense—not a lot, but *more* than a lot. But a plethora of people are still using the word as if it simply means "many." Just recently we heard someone say that there were a plethora of good ideas at the meeting he attended. Did he mean there were too many good ideas?

poinsettia

[poin-SET-ee-uh]

*red and green foliaged plant of the Spurge family,
most often used in Christmas floral displays*

According to Dora Fleming of the *Gwinnett Daily Post*,
"Sixty-one million poinsettias were purchased in the United
States [last year]. Of this number, probably at least sixty
million people mispronounced the name of the plant they
took home."

Those sixty million probably said "point-SET-a" when
it's actually pronounced "poin-SET-ee-uh." But it's so often
mispronounced that a number of dictionaries now include
the incorrect pronunciation as well. It is named after Joel
Roberts Poinsett, the first United States Minister to Mexico,
who brought the pretty plant into the United States in 1825.

Why is the *ia* tacked on to Mr. Poinsett's name? It's a
normal convention in plant or animal naming, as in *wisteria*,
named after a certain Mr. Wistar or Wister. Other times
scientists add an *i* or *ae* to names of people they wish to
honor—and so we have *Agaporomorphus colberti*, a beetle
named after Stephen Colbert, *Kootenichela deppi, an* extinct
arthropod named after Johnny Depp, and who can forget
Scaptia beyonceae, a biting horsefly named after Beyonce?

prerogative

[pri-ROG-uh-tiv]

noun: an official or hereditary right or privilege that gives its possessor an advantage over others; adjective: having a hereditary or official right or privilege

Herewith is the flip side to *peremptory*—in that many people transpose the (correct) "pre" into the (incorrect) "per," pronouncing it *"per*-ROG-uh-tiv" rather than *"pri*-ROG-uh-tiv." Yes, it's yet another example of a metathesis, and, yes, it's an extremely common mistake.

It comes from the Latin (of course) *praerogātīva* (initially meaning "previous verdict, claim, and privilege," and later also meaning "superiority and a special right or privilege exercised by the monarch"). And, as you can see, it hasn't really changed all that much over the centuries. It appears in very similar form in other languages through time as well—there's the thirteenth-century Old French *prérogative,* the fourteenth-century Catalan *prerrogativa*, the fifteenth-century Spanish and Portuguese *prerrogativa* or *prerogativa,* and the fifteenth-century Italian *prerogativa*. The meaning of the word, similarly, didn't change much over the years. And presumably (not persumably!) the pronunciation remained similar . . . and so easy to mispronounce.

prestigious

[preh-STIJ-us]

having prestige, being honored

Prestigious comes from the classical Latin *praestīgiōsus*, meaning "full of tricks, deceitful" (which was the first, now obsolete, meaning of the word). And it can be a tricky word indeed. It's a small thing, literally and figuratively, that makes *prestigious* a shibboleth word for so many: the letter *i*; actually, both of them. The first *i* is not pronounced *ee*, and the second *i* is elided over, not emphasized. This makes the preferred pronunciation "preh-STIJ-us," not "preh-STEE-jus" or, even worse, "preh-STEE-gee-us."

This is an easy error to make, since the *i* in *prestige* is pronounced as a long *e*. And in so many other words, you pronounce the *i* in the "ious" (*devious*, etc.) But, of course, these pronunciations don't apply to *prestigious*.

In their *Elements of Style*, Strunk and White say that *prestigious* is "often an adjective of last resort. It's in the dictionary, but that doesn't mean you have to use it." We don't agree. Feel free to use *prestigious* . . . but not "pres-TEE-gee-us."

preventive

[pri-VEN-tiv]

something that prevents something, especially disease, as in preventive medicine

Many of us say "pre-VEN-ta-tive" instead of "pre-VEN-tive," and while it's not technically wrong, the *OED* says that the original adjective is *preventive,* and in its delightfully understated way says of *preventative*: "Avoidance of the present word and the use in its place of preventive n. and preventive adj. is recommended by some usage guides." Count us among them.

Just to muddy the linguistic waters, both *preventive* and *preventative* are actually about the same age, so neither really takes linguistic precedence. The *Merriam-Webster Dictionary* lists *preventative* (used in the same sense as *preventive*) as being first used circa 1666, and lists *preventive* as first used around 1639. Similarly, a close look at *OED* citations also shows that there's only a thirty-year difference. So even if *preventive* was used first, it was only barely so.

So what should we say, then? Take a look at the computer and see what people are using. According to the Google Ngram Viewer, which shows how often a word is used in print, *preventive* is used more than three times as frequently as *preventative*—as of 2013. So *preventive* it is.

prostrate

[PROS-trayt]

to lie face down; to bow down or lie with one's face on the ground in a gesture of submission or obsequiousness

Prostrate is not in and of itself difficult to pronounce. But it is a shibboleth word because it is so often confused with *prostate*, the male gland that produces seminal fluid. This gland, of course, has nothing to do with lying face down or bowing before royalty. Someone theoretically could be prostrate due to his prostate, but that's as close as the two words get.

You might think the *prostrate-prostate* confusion is a newish one, springing from modern grammatical sloppiness, but actually *prostrate* has been misused for centuries. Back in 1686, one C. Peter wrote about "prostrate glandules" in his *Observations on Venereal Disease*. Similarly, in the 1700s and 1800s, scientific articles and books (such as the excitingly titled "A description of the human urinary bladder, and parts belonging to it: with anatomical figures") referred to "prostrate glands." It's an error that continues to be made, but as the Happy Hospitalist website for health professionals put it: "Stop calling your prostate your prostrate. What the fruck is wrong with you?"

pwn

[pohn]

*in computer gaming, to be dominated or
beaten by an opponent to a humiliating degree;
now extended to being humiliated or dominated
in noncomputer areas as well*

The vowel-less *pwn* looks like one of those Welsh
words that has consonants smashed together and seems
unpronounceable. But it's an American word, one born
in the computer age, and one that looks like it's missing a
vowel because it *is* missing a vowel. It is, according to most
explanations of its origin, a misspelling of the word *own*—
occurring because on a QWERTY keyboard, the *o* and *p* are
next to one another.

There is debate, though, as to who misspelled "own" as
"pwn" and thus launched the word. Some people say it was
a common typo occurring when hackers talked about taking
remote control of a network or server and they meant to type
"owning" the network. Others say it can be traced back to one
of the designers on the computer game *Warcraft*. When the
computer beat a player, a message saying that you "have been
owned" was supposed to pop up. But he typed it incorrectly,
and the message instead said you "have been pwned."

Whatever its background, *pwn* caught on with gamers
and other computer-related groups and now has spread
into regular slang usage. One could say the word pwnd the
English language to some degree.

quay

[kee]

a platform or structure (typically stone or concrete)
built next to a river, lake, or ocean used for loading
and unloading freight and passengers; wharf; jetty

In *quay* we have another example of the particularly irritating nautical words that look so easy to pronounce, but are, of course, pronounced quite differently than they are spelled. *Quay* looks like it should be "kway," of course. But somehow, along the line, *quay* lost its logical pronunciation.

If you trace the word back to its roots, its genealogical antecedent was pronounced more the way you'd think *quay* should be pronounced but isn't. *Quay* evolved from *kay*, the Old French word that was probably of Gaulish origin but evolved into the Middle English *key*. In the late seventeenth century, the spelling changed, influenced by the contemporary French spelling *quai*, to *quay* . . . but still pronounced "key."

So are the Florida Keys actually the Florida Quays? It sounds nice and neat, but no, they're not. The Keys got their name from the Spanish word for small island—*cayo*. This probably came from the same root as the French *kay*, but instead of evolving into *quay*, *cayo* evolved into *key* and stayed there. It also evolved into *cay* (also pronounced "key"), which is defined as a small island or, yes, a key.

quinoa

[KEEN-wah]

*the small protein-rich seeds of the tall annual
goosefoot plant, originally cultivated as a food plant
in parts of the Andes and now grown more widely*

Another of the most mispronounced food words, *quinoa*
looks not like "KEEN-wah," but like it should be pronounced
"KWIN-oh-ah" or "kwin-OH-a," which is what many people
say when they've only read the word and not heard it (one of
whom is writing this . . .).

You'd be forgiven if you thought quinoa was a fairly
recent discovery, since it has been only over the past decade
that you can't avoid seeing quinoa on menus, in pricey
specialty stores, in cereals, muffins, . . . anything. But it's an
old, old food plant, cultivated in the Andes for centuries, and
written about in the English language since the latter 1500s.
For example, in 1598, we have Jan Huygen van Linschoten
making note of "A kinde of fruit called Quinua . . . wherof
they make their drinke, and eate it . . . as we do rice."

Quinua was the earlier South American Spanish version
of the Quechua *kinuwa* (sometimes spelled *kinwa*)—and if
you know Spanish, you can see why it is still pronounced the
way it is. And even if you don't know Spanish, you can now
be healthy without making anyone snicker when you ask for
it at your local market.

remuneration

[ri-MYOO-nuh-ray-shuhn]

payment received for work or service done

With this shibboleth word, the temptation is to flip the *m* and the *n* and say "re-NOOM-err-ay-shuhn" instead of the correct "ri-MYOO-nuh-ray-shuhn." This letter switching (or metathesis, see page 15) possibly happens because you're thinking of numbers when you're thinking about payments and "num" seems appropriate. Or it could simply be that we're more used to saying "noo" than "myoo" in the middle of a word. But whatever the reason, it's an extremely common problem.

In fact, *remuneration* was among the top ten words most difficult to pronounce in a 2012 study conducted by the British Institute of Verbatim Reporters; and in a study conducted by voicemail-to-text conversion company Spinvox, it was named the third most commonly mispronounced word.

It might help to be aware that the word did not come from the same root as *number* but evolved from the Latin word *munus* (civic duties), from which we get the words *municipal* and *immunity,* both having the "myoo" sound. Interestingly, we have noted that while so many people have trouble pronouncing *remuneration*, they have absolutely no trouble accepting it.

HOW TO SOUND LIKE AN OENOPHILE

The Seventeen Wines (and One Wine Steward) Most Commonly Mispronounced

cabernet sauvignon: CAB-er-nay soh-vin-YOH(n)
(with a soft *n*)

gewurztraminer: geh-VERTS-truh-meen-er

grenache: gruh-NOSH

montepulciano d'Abruzzo:
mon-tay-pul-chee-AH-noh dah-BRUTE-so

moscato: moh-SKAH-toh

muscadet: moos-kah-DAY

pinot noir: PEE-noh nwar

riesling: REECE-ling

rioja: ree-OH-hah

sangiovese: san-jo-VAY-zee

sauvignon blanc: SOH-vin-yoh(n) blohnk (with a soft *n*)

semillon: seh-mee-YHO(n) (with a soft *n*)

shiraz: shih-RAHZ or shih-RAHS

sommelier: sawm-uh-I-YAY

syrah: see-RAH

tempranillo: tem-prah-NEE-yoh

vinho verde: VEEN-yo VAYR-deh

zinfandel: ZIN-fuhn-del

restaurateur

[res-ter-uh-TOOR]

a person who owns and/or manages a restaurant

The temptation with this word—from the French, of course—is to take *restaurant* and simply add an "eur" to it. *Restauranteur*: It rolls off the tongue. It seems simple. It seems *right*. But it's (technically) wrong.

Restaurateur has no *n* in it, probably because it originally came from the classical Latin *restaurator*. It's "rat," not "rant." (We'd say there's an easy mnemonic for this—something along the lines of "put the 'rat' back in *restaurateur*"—but that doesn't seem fair to the non-vermin-infested restaurant owners out there.)

As for the problematic *restauranteur*, it has actually been misspelled and mispronounced for quite a long time. The *Oxford English Dictionary* notes that it is an American invention and finds examples dating back to 1859. But its usage didn't really catch on until the twentieth century. Now its prevalence has led it to be accepted and even included in some dictionaries, but it's still considered quite indigestible by many.

schadenfreude

[SHAH-den-froy-duh]

*enjoyment or pleasure from hearing or
seeing the troubles of other people*

Schadenfreude is one of those useful words from another language that is used because there's no equivalent in our own. In the Tony Award–winning musical *Avenue Q*, it's defined succinctly as "Schadenfreude, makin' me feel glad that I'm not you!" "To gloat" is close but doesn't quite catch the meaning. The most popular English dictionary of the 1700s, Nathan Bailey's *An* [sic] *Universal Etymological English Dictionary*, had an English entry, *epicharikaky*, derived from the ancient Greek, that was probably the closest English equivalent to *schadenfreude*. But for obvious reasons, it didn't catch on (just try saying "epicharikaky" out loud). So "SHAH-den-froy-duh" with the "duh" at the end it is.

Unfortunately, many people leave off the last "duh" sound. This prompted someone on Twitter to give a new definition for *schadenfreude*: "The pleasure of seeing other people mispronounce German words."

segue

[SEG-way]

to move smoothly and without interruption from one musical piece, film scene, conversational topic, and so on, to another, or (as a noun) a smooth transition from one song, and so on, to another

This is one of those words that many people recognize in speech but don't recognize in writing and for good reason: "segue" looks like it should be "SEE-goo" or "SHE-gyoo" or anything other than "SEG-way."

"Why isn't it like *vogue*, which as far as I know isn't pronounced 'vogway'?" you may be thinking in an internal dialogue ("dialogway"?). Let's pursue (not "pursway") this. The not-so-phonetic-to-us spelling is due to *segue*'s origins. It evolved from the Italian *seguire* (to follow—and pronounced "seh-GWEE-ray"), which in turn came from the Latin *sequi* (to follow or come after—pronounced "SEH-kwee"). Unlike the French *vogue* and *pursue*, *segue* has the lilting Italian sound, which is fitting since it was originally used in musical scores. The word wasn't used to denote an uninterrupted transition in other ways until 1937 and wasn't used as a noun until the 1950s.

So "SEG-way" it is, pronounced like the name of the transport device that was supposed to become the personal vehicle of choice for all, but, well, didn't.

settee

[set-TEE]

*a long seat with a back and (usually) arms
for holding two or more people*

This word makes many people fall into the old "it looks like it might be French, so let me say it as if it is" trap. They say "set-TAY" (not to be confused with "SA-tay," which you eat rather than sit upon), thinking they're adding French flair to it. But *settee* isn't French at all . . . which is why the *ee* suffix is plain old "ee" as in "Eek, you pronounced that incorrectly."

In fact, the word *settee* appears to be a purely English invention that first emerged in the early 1700s. No one is completely sure where it came from, although it probably was just a variation on the word *settle,* which also meant "seat." In the UK, the first syllable is stressed as in *settle,* so it's "SET-tee." But for some reason, it has become "set-TEE" in the United States.

One final note: There is another older meaning for *settee* that is not as widely used nowadays. This *settee,* derived from *seatta,* the Italian word for "arrow," dates back to the late 1500s. And this one can cause confusion to the modern reader who runs across mention of a settee going out to sea. Just to make things perfectly clear: This settee is a boat with a long prow and two or three masts. It is *not* a peculiar amphibious couch.

sherbet

[SHUR-bit]

frozen dessert of fruit juice, water,
sugar, and usually cream

Sherbet doesn't rhyme with Herbert. But for some reason (and no one really knows why), many people throw an extra *r* into the word, possibly because it somehow sounds more "right."

A recent Google Ngram Viewer chart found 160,000 usages for *sherbet* and 28,500 for *sherbert*. That's one in six people *writing* the word *sherbet* incorrectly. Many more *say* it with that extra *r*. *Sherbet* has been spelled many different ways in English over the years—*zerbet, cerbet, shurbet, sherpet, sherbette*, and *sarbet*—but notice there's no *rt* ending among them.

The word came to English from the Arabic *shariba* (to drink) by way of Turkish and Persian *sherbet*. The early English traveler Sandys marveled at "the costly Shurbets of Constantinople" in 1615. Soon the concoction of iced fruits and sugar entered European cuisines . . . and European vocabularies. Along the way, dairy was added to the fruit and sugar, which often is a distinction between it and the related dessert *sorbet* (which has the same word origin as *sherbet*). So sorbet is actually the traditional sherbet, since it typically has no added dairy . . . and no added *r* either. No one ever calls it *sorbert*.

sidereal

[sye-DEER-ee-uhl]

of the stars; usually referring to a timescale that is based on Earth's rate of rotation measured relative to the fixed stars rather than the sun

Astronomers and astrologers, who so often disagree about the meaning of the stars, at least agree on the pronunciation of this commonly mispronounced word. It's never "side-reel."

That is because it is not a compound word—*side* and *real*—but an adjective derived from the Latin word for constellation or star: *sidus*. English took the Latin adjective of *sidus*, *sīdereus* (of the stars) and chopped off the *us* and then added an English-sounding "-all" (actually an Anglo-Norman *al* adjectival suffix).

Sometimes the *i* was replaced with an Old English–looking *y*, to make *sydereall*, which looked pretty much how it is pronounced today. But over the years, the *y* reverted back to the original *i* and one of the *l*'s was unfortunately lost to make *sidereal*. Chances are that back in Shakespearean times, people rarely mispronounced *sydereall*, the spelling of which at least gives you a clue about its pronunciation. The modern spelling is trickier—and, in our opinion, much uglier.

Siobhan

[shih-VAWN]

Irish woman's name meaning "God is gracious"

When it comes to Irish, it's Greek to us. It is packed with words that look completely different from how they're said. Take the name *Siobhan.*

Anyone who isn't Irish or who doesn't already know how it's pronounced would (logically) think it is "SIGH-oh-bahn" or perhaps "SEE-ohb-han." They would not make an amazing leap and say, "Of course. It's Shivawn!"

Irish has several differences with other European languages. For example, in this case, we can see the Irish phonetic rule wherein an *s* before an *i* or an *e* has a *sh* sound, and a *bh* (or, for that matter, an *mh*) is pronounced as a *v* (sometimes as a *w* if it is in the middle of a word but not the beginning, but that's another story).

And just in case it all seems nice and clear now, look at the other ways you can spell Siobahn:

Chevon, Chevone, Chevonne, Chivonne, Chivoun, Ciobhinne, Shavaughan, Shavaughn, Shavaughne, Shavaugn, Shavaugne, Shavaun, Shavaune, Shavon, Shavone, Shavonne, Sheavaughn, Shevaun, Shevawn, Shevonne, Shievonne, Shivan, Shivaughn, Shivaughne, Shivaun, Shivaune, Shivon, Shivonne, Shvaugn, Siavon, Siobahn, Siobain, Sioban, Siobhain, Siobhann, Siobhin, Siobhon, Siovhan, and Siubhan.

Just be glad we didn't write about *Niamh* . . . which is pronounced "neeve," if you can beliamh it.

slough

[sloo], [slow] (rhymes with cow), [sluff]

noun: a marshy boggy area; verb: to shed skin;
noun: skin that has been shed

With *slough*, we face the "ough" conundrum: Does it rhyme with rough, cough, through, or bough? It's enough to make you through—we mean, throw—up your hands.

It depends upon which *kind* of slough you are referring to. The boggy *slough* is "sloo" or "slow." It comes from the Old English *sloh* (which dates back to 900), which would make one assume that "slow" would be preferred, but while it is accepted, in the United States, the "sloos" usually have it. In fact, in the United States and Canada, it is sometimes spelled "slew."

The skin *slough* is "sluff," and it's newer, dating back to the 1300s. It is pronounced differently probably because it came from the low German word for husking or peeling, *sluwe*. Over time this *slough* was pronounced "sluff"—and has even been spelled that way.

We can complicate matters more by tossing in yet another *slew*—the informal word meaning "a large number," as in "there are a slew of ways to pronounce *slough*." This *slew* is a completely unrelated word that originated in nineteenth-century America and probably came from the Irish word for crowd (*slua* or *sluagh*), so it has nothing to do with sloughs of any meaning. Phew.

sough

[suff] (also sow)

rushing, rustling, or murmuring sound, as in wind soughing; geographically, a boggy place

Soule's Pronouncing Handbook is explicit: *Sough* is "suff" and that is that. But *Soule's* was written in 1873 when *sough* was an up-and-coming word. Actually, sough was a *number* of words, some older than others. But today there are usually only two soughs you might run across. And in both cases, "sow" (which rhymes with "cow") has also become acceptable.

The rather prosaic boggy-drainage-ditch *sough* comes from the Middle English *sogh,* possibly from the Dutch *zoeg* (little ditch). You probably won't run across this word much unless you're into geography.

As for the rustling, murmuring *sough*, it too comes from Middle English, but from *swoh* or *swog* from the Old English *swogan* (to resound or sound). Other than in Scots and Northern dialect, it wasn't used that much from the sixteenth century until the nineteenth century when it became a popular word in literature. It has fallen from popularity again, though, and you'll rarely encounter it outside of old literature—which is a shame as it's so evocative. Take this passage from I. L. Bird's *A Lady's Life in the Rocky Mountains,* written in 1879: "The strange sough of gusts moving among the pine tops." Maybe it's time to bring it back again . . . ?

[spit and IM-ij]

exact likeness, look-alike, doppelganger, duplicate

No, we didn't mean to type "spitting image." The phrase is three words—"spit and image"—and it is one of the most common shibboleth phrases both in speech and in print. "Spitting image" trounces "spit and image" in the usage stakes. "Spitting image" was used almost seventeen times more often in print than "spit and image" when we did a Google Ngram Viewer search, while a Google search found over one million listings for "spitting image," and only about 23,500 for "spit and image."

But "spit and image" most linguists say it is (technically), even if it's highly likely that you'll be corrected by people if you use it. (One caveat: Yale linguist Laurence Horn believes the original phrase was "spitten image"—with spit standing in for another, stickier bodily fluid.)

Some say the "spit and image" comes from a black magic or voodoo ceremony; others say it evolved from "*spirit* and image." And still others say it is biblical in origin— referring to God using spit and mud to make Adam in his own image. Regardless of the actual roots, "spit and image" begat "spitten image," which begat "spitting image"—which is where we are today . . . even if it *really* should be "spit and image."

spurious

[SPYOOR-ee-us]

fake or false, not what it should be

Spurious should have a soft "yoo" sound just after the *sp*. Think of how you pronounce the *u* (or how you *should* pronounce the *u*) in *spume*.

It comes from a late Latin word *spurius*, which meant "born out of wedlock"—which some say came from the precursors of the Romans, the mysterious Etruscans, and their word *spural*, which meant "public." The Romans took over the word (and, for that matter, the Etruscans), and by late Imperial times had their word *spurius* referring to illegitimate children.

By the 1600s, *spurious* had expanded in scope to mean more than merely illegitimacy in the birth sense. With the English ending "ous" substituted for the Latin ending "ius," it came to mean anything or anyone fake, false, or not what it should be . . . as in this two-word phrase (used by mathematicians and computer scientists) we had never encountered before: a *spurious tuple* (the *u* in *tuple* is pronounced with the same soft "yoo" sound as in *spurious*), which is basically a false record in a database or set that gets created by the incorrect joining of two tables.

How's that for some spuriously useful information for most of us?

supposedly

[sup-POSE-ed-lee]

*according to what is believed or assumed,
often without conclusive evidence*

Yes, this word is pronounced exactly as it is written, but it is still a shibboleth word. It is included in this collection because some people seem to think the word is *supposably*. And, as you might expect, some people are wrong.

Supposably is the adverb form of *supposable*, so it means "capable of being supposed," or more succinctly, "conceivable." This is a very different thing than "according to what is believed"—and why you can't just toss in a *supposably* when you actually mean *supposedly*. Yet people (primarily Americans) persist in this. According to a 2015 study released by Dictionary.com, over one-third of Americans say they have heard people using *supposably* when they meant *supposedly*. But while Americans use it, the word itself originated in England in the late eighteenth century. The Brits don't really regard *supposably* as a legit word these days and tend to view it more as American vernacular. In fact, even in the United States, it is rare to find *supposably* used as it should be. It seems to be more of a quasi word, or more precisely a real word that no one uses in the real way . . . supposedly.

synecdoche

[sin-NECK-duh-kee]

a figure of speech in which one uses the name of a part to represent the whole, and vice versa, or the material a thing is made from for the thing itself

This is one of those smart-looking shibboleth words that you run across in articles and books. And if you're like many people, not only are you unsure how it's pronounced, you're also a bit unsure what it *is*. You just know it looks pretty cool.

Even if you are a little vague as to what synecdoches are, you've probably been using them frequently. For example, if you've talked about "the White House" announcing something, discussed a sports team by saying the name of the city rather than the team ("Seattle's O-line"), or mentioned an actor treading the boards instead of being on stage, you've used synedoches.

The term (and the trope) has been used since the thirteenth century and hasn't really changed much over that time. It evolved from the classical Latin *synedoche*, from the Greek *synekdokhe* (which is spelled much more like the word is pronounced), meaning "receiving something from another." In the fourteenth and fifteenth centuries, it became *synecdoque* in French, *sinécdoque* in Spanish, *sineddoche* in Italian, and *synekdoche* in German. All very simple for a word that looks so smart!

And speaking of smart . . . are you smart enough to answer this quick extra credit question: What U.S. city rhymes with *synecdoche*?

tenet

[TEN-it]

a principle, a belief, especially relating to religion or philosophy

A tenet is a belief; a tenant is someone who rents an apartment from a landlord. Thousands of people confuse the two, throw in an extra *n*, and say *tenant* for *tenet*. (Fortunately, no one seems to confuse it the other way.) It's a mistake found not just in speech, but in print also. Do a quick search on Google books and you'll find many examples of this confusion, including many in books by major publishers, such as this in the prestigious academic publisher Springer Publishing's *Encyclopedia of Psychology and Religion:* "Irvin Yalom, noted American existential psychiatrist, would agree that death anxiety is a basic tenant of human existence." Unless death anxiety is renting space from human existence, this is wrong.

Interestingly, *tenet* in early English was written with an *n*—*tenent*—but by the 1500s, the second *n* was gone . . . as it should be from all of our pronunciations. And that's a basic tenet of this book.

on tenterhooks

[on TEN-ter hooks]

in a state of anxious suspense, uneasy anticipation

We could say that you're a cliché tenderfoot if you, like many other people, say someone is "on *tender*hooks." But we won't since nowadays a lot of people don't know what *tenderfoot* means (a novice). Even fewer know what *tenterhooks* means, including those who know it's the right word in this shibboleth phrase.

This is probably because the word refers to an outmoded device used in medieval times—a *tenter*, a frame for keeping cloth stretched as it dries so it doesn't shrink. Tenterhooks are the small hooks or pins on the frame that held the cloth. So someone uneasily anticipating something is stretched like the fabric.

This unfamiliar word is probably why "on tenterhooks" lands on numerous "phrases people most often misquote" lists. It made the top ten listing of most often misquoted sayings in Britain. But while we've heard otherwise intelligent and well-spoken people *saying* "tenderhooks," it isn't an error made often in print.

HOW TO SOUND LIKE A GOURMET

The Twenty-Eight Food Names Even Foodies Often Get Wrong

bánh mì: bahn MEE

beignet: ben-YAY

calzone: cal-ZOH-nee, cal-ZOH-ney

charcuterie: shahr-KOO-tuhr-ee or shar-koo-tuhr-EE

crème fraîche: CREM fresh

jicama: HEE-kuh-muh

kefir: kuh-FEER

lardons: lahr-DOH(n)

macaroon: mak-uh-RUH(n)

maraschino: mar-uh-SKEEN-oh

niçoise: nee-SWAHZ

prosciutto: proh-SHOO-toh

provolone: proh-vuh-LOH-nee

radicchio: rah-DEE-kee-oh

raita: rah-YEE-tah

rillettes: ree-YEHT or rih-LEHTS

tagliatelle: ta-yuh-TEL-ee

tournedos: TOOR-ni-doh or toor-nuh-DOH

tzatziki: dzah-DZEE-kee

Thames

[tems]

name of the largest river in England, which flows past London and Oxford; also the name of rivers in Connecticut and Ontario

Londoners might call it "the River," but the rest of us should know that it's "tems," not "thaymes," in spite of the *th*.

The name probably comes from the old Celtic word *tamesas*, meaning "dark." When the Romans conquered England, they called it Tamesis. So where did the *th* come in? It's most likely the same old story: learned pedants were trying to make the name sound more like it came from their beloved ancient classical authors. In this case, they got even more persnickety; preferring the Greek *th* over the Latin *t*. The first recorded spelling of *Thames* with a *th* comes from 1649; the *th* may have been added to sound like the River Thyamis in Greece. (The pedants gave the *th* treatment to Marc Antony too, yielding "Marc Anthony.")

A more amusing but far less credible story has it that when one of the originally German-speaking Georges took the British throne, he couldn't pronounce the English *th*, so the entire court, and then the entire country, pronounced the river as "tems" to preserve his royal dignity.

One final note: If you visit the *other* River Thames (in Connecticut), yes, call it the "thaymes."

theater

[THEE-uh-ter]

a building used for performances;
originally just referring to plays

The chief problem with *theater* is that little second syllable, that seemingly innocuous *a*. Some people sort of ignore it, and, in an eliding way, say "THEEr-ter," with a soft *r* taking the place of the entire second syllable. Others turn the syllable into a long *a* sound and, to make matters worse, put the stress on it: "thee-AY-ter." According to Dictionary.com, this last pronunciation is "characteristic chiefly of uneducated speech."

But if you're one of these "uneducated" churls who does that (one of us is), you can point out to whomever corrects you that, as with so many pronunciations that are now sneered at, this was actually the original way to say it in Middle English, since it came from the French *theatre*, pronounced "tey-AH-truh." (Prior to that, it was the Latin *theatrum* from the Greek *theatron*.) But as with many other words that came from the French (such as *carriage* and *marriage*), the second syllable stress switched to the first. Not very dramatic, but that's the story.

timbre

[TAM-ber]

quality of a sound; combination of qualities of a sound that distinguishes it from other sounds of the same pitch and volume

Ask some musicians: most will pronounce *timbre* with an *a* sound, rhyming it with *amber*. Ask some doctors, and many will pronounce it "timber." What to do?

We say "TAM-ber" because it's the original English pronunciation. And while many dictionaries, such as *Merriam-Webster*, the *OED*, and *Cambridge,* list the "timber" pronunciation, "TAM-ber" is the first listed. The word came to English from the French by way of Latin and Greek words with somewhat different meanings. By the time of the French medieval period, *timbre* meant a small bell, and then the meaning came to include the sound of the bell, and from there, the current definition. So, traditionally, *timbre* has the French-sounding pronunciation in which the *i* sounds like an *a*. (Note that the *re* ending is *not* pronounced as a Frenchman would.) So say "TAM-ber" and save "tim-ber" for yelling out when you chop down a tree.

Tolkien (J. R. R.)

[TOLL-keen]

author of The Hobbit *and* The Lord of the Rings *trilogy*

Most readers automatically know his name . . . and pronounce it either "TOLL-ken" or "TOLL-kin." We've always been in the "TOLL-ken" camp since we first read his works as kids, and only in doing this book did we learn we've been wrong all these years.

Neither pronunciation is right. J. R. R. himself said it's "TOLL-keen." As he wrote in a letter:

> *I am nearly always written to as Tolkein (not by you): I do not know why, since it is pronounced by me always as keen.*

So that's that, right? Well . . . not quite. Recorded interviews with Tolkien's descendants have them pronouncing it slightly differently—"TOLL-kee-en." But the "kee" and the "en" are blurred together, so it's almost "TOLL-keen," but with a hint of a third syllable . . . which sounds almost as complicated as Elvish.

triathlon

[tri-ATH-luhn]

athletic contest consisting of three different endurance events, usually swimming, cycling, and long-distance running

It's hard leaving out the (wrong) extra *a* in *triathlon*. It's up there with *athlete* and *arthritis*, both of which almost compel some people to throw in an extra *a*. For *triathlon* in particular, it sounds more natural, even though it's clearly wrong and the spelling tells us so. The "thlo" combination is very rare in English and sounds extremely unnatural. In fact, except for the related words *biathlon*, *pentathlon*, and so on, we found only one theoretically common bona fide English word with "thlo" in it (besides companies with Earthlog brands): *arithlog*. What's an arithlog? It's semilogarithmic coordinate paper, and we're sure you use it every day.

Just remember that "athlon" is the root word here. It meant "contest" in ancient Greek, so with the modern Olympics, in honor of the Greeks, multipart athletic contests were called "athlons" with a word signifying how many parts put in front as a prefix—that is, "bi-athlons" for two-part events, "tri-athlons" for three-part ones, and so on—all the way up to "dec-athlons."

trompe l'oeil

[tromp-LOY]

artistic technique in which a flat surface is painted to appear deceptively three-dimensional

Trompe l'oeil—which literally means "deceives the eye" in French—is one of those French words that also deceives English speakers who try to pronounce it. Many of them see the *l* and say something like "tromp loyal." Or they see the "oei" vowel string and just mumble.

It should sound like an *oe* that slips into the *ee* sound in one smooth syllable. Even though the French plural of *eye* is *yeux*, never say "trompe les yeux"—just say "trompe l'oiels," or "trompe l'oeil," for both the singular and plural, just like the French.

And don't be deceived by people saying "trompe *d'*oeil"— which literally means "deceives *of* eye," which doesn't make too much sense, deceptive or otherwise. It's surprisingly not that uncommon, though. We found it in numerous art books, gallery flyers, and theater websites.

turmeric

[TUR-mer-ik]

bright yellow powdered root spice, especially prevalent in Asian cuisines, also used as a yellow dye; the tropical plant itself

When it comes to this shibboleth word, there's one thing that immediately comes to mind: Arr! ARR! No, we are not pretending to be pirates but are referring to the oft-overlooked *r* in *turmeric* that results in people saying "too-mer-ik."

Interestingly, while the *r* is sometimes missing in pronunciation, there actually was once a *t* that is now missing from the spelling. While *turmeric*'s origin is "obscure," to use the *OED* term, it does appear to have initially been spelled *tarmaret* (as found in a 1545 custom house rate book listing), *tormarith* (in a 1582 custom house listing), and *turmeryte* (early 1600s). It might have come from the Middle French for saffron (*terremérite*) via the medieval Latin *terra merita*, "deserving or worthy earth," but no one is positive. It is similarly unclear about how and why the *t* became a *c*. It's possible it was just a spelling error that persisted, or an evolution due to the influence of other words like *arsenic*. Some have even speculated that it came from the spelling of saffron (the Persian-Arabic *kurkum*, which led to the Latin *curcuma*).

So no one is really sure about many things where turmeric is concerned. But the *r*? That they're sure about.

utmost

[UT-most]

at the farthest limit; the greatest extent or amount

It requires absolutely no imagination to deduce the correct pronunciation of this word. But it is included in this collection of shibboleth words because so many people persist in pronouncing it "UP-most." In fact, it is one of the one hundred most commonly mispronounced words in English.

To make matters more confusing, there actually *is* a word *upmost*—but not only does it mean something completely different than *utmost*, it also has evolved in American English into *uppermost*. (They still use *upmost* in the UK, but that's not of the utmost importance to us here.)

Uppermost means highest in rank and/or position. *Utmost* means the highest or greatest degree. So on one hand, you have the uppermost or upmost rung on a ladder; on the other, the utmost care taken in climbing to that high rung.

So *up* has nothing to do with *utmost*. It is *ut* and has been since the early 900s. It derives from the Middle English *utmest—out-most*, or *outermost*. And since then it takes the utmost of patience to hear people say "upmost." Perhaps they should keep the notion of "out" uppermost in their minds?

Uranus

[YOOR-uh-nuss]

the seventh planet from the sun; ancient Greek god

"Can I have a look at Uranus too, Lavender?" asked Ron in *Harry Potter and the Goblet of Fire*—and because of snickery sentences like this the preferred pronunciation of Uranus has changed from "yoor-AY-nus" to "YOOR-uh-nuss," with the emphasis on the "yoor" and a tasteful avoidance of emphasizing the problematic "anus."

The word *Uranus* is actually the Latin (and later the English) deity name originally from the ancient Greek *Ouranós*, with an accent on both the first and last syllables. But pronouncing as the Greeks did would sound very odd in English. To the ancient Greeks, Ouranos or Uranus was the earliest god of the heavens; but to us, it's that giant blue planet, the seventh planet from the sun. Uranus was discovered to be a planet in 1781 by the astronomer Sir William Herschel. (Up to then people thought it was a star or comet.) The entire mispronunciation problem with Uranus could have been entirely avoided: Herschel wanted to name his new discovery "Georgium Sidus," the Georgian Planet, in honor of King George III of England. You can't make too many jokes with a planetary name like that.

van Gogh (Vincent)

[van GOKH] (or [van KOKH])

artist

For a long time, the debate has raged here in America: If you want to sound like a true art aficionado, do you say "van GO," "van GOG," or "van GOFF"? The definitive answer: It's none of the above.

In fact, it's virtually impossible for those of us who don't speak Dutch to say Vincent van Gogh's name correctly. In Dutch, it would be more like "vun kHOKH" or possibly "fun kHOKH," with the beginning *kH* more like a plain *H* with a teeny bit of aspiration and the last *KH* like a gutteral *gh* sound. It's a sound the English language doesn't really have.

So because English isn't Dutch and it's difficult to get the sounds quite right, most English speakers (including the venerable BBC in their official pronunciation guidelines that ensure that everyone on "the Beeb" says things the same way) opt for "van GOKH" as the closest approximation, with some semipurists choosing "van KOKH."

Of course, though, since we've all been saying "van GO" forever, there's the danger of sounding a tad pretentious when you go for the "van GOKH." Our advice: There's no harm in sticking with the tried and true. You can always *say* you know it's pronounced differently, but it grates on your ear. (Ouch.)

vehicle

[VEE-i-kuhl]

a thing used to transmit or transport something

If you want to sound smart, we vehemently say don't pronounce the *h* in *vehicle* (or in *vehement*, for that matter). Most grammarians eschew the *h*, and, yes, the authoritative *Fowler's Modern English Usage* says "in Standard English now, the *h* is never pronounced." But pronouncing it with the *h* is not considered incorrect, just maybe a bit hickey (and icky too).

It wasn't always that way. Educated people in the 1800s were almost always told to say "VEE-hik-cal" with a distinct *h*. Oglivie's *The Student's English Dictionary* (1865) (with the "pronunciation adapted to the best modern usage") clearly favored sounding the *h*. So did *Cooley's Dictionary* (1861), Soule and Wheeler's *Manual of English Pronunciation* (1882), and *Funk and Wagnall's Standard* (1897). Since the original Latin word was *vehiculum*, the old Romans also probably pronounced the *h*, too.

So why now no *h*? Who the h knows? For some reason, over the next hundred years, the accepted pronunciation changed, and now, for better or worse, the *h* has departed from polite company.

vichyssoise

[vee-shee-SWHAZ] or [vi-shee-SWHAZ]

a French leek and potato soup, usually served cold

We include this soup because our mother (like millions of others) has always insisted on mispronouncing it as "vee-shee-SWA" and not as it should sound—"vee-" or "vi-sh-SWHAZ." This shibboleth is a famous example of another hyperforeignism, which, as we mentioned before (see page 39) happens when people take loan words from other languages and blithely apply what they think are the rules of that language to those words. They're usually incorrect, since they usually don't speak the other languages.

Vichyssoise is probably mispronounced as "vee-shee-SWA" by our soup-making mom and others because they've heard that the French very often don't pronounce the last sounds of written words (as in *haricot vert*, see page 74). But the French do pronounce the final part of "oise" words. That "oise" has a characteristically French "waz" sound that only the French can really say. Interestingly, there is another word in English that comes from French Revolutionary and later Marxist times that also has that "waz" sound—*bourgeoisie*—meaning middle classes . . . those people who, we assume, were avid consumers of vichyssoise soup.

victual

[VIT-l]

food, provisions for consumption

In the hit 1960s TV show *The Beverly Hillbillies*, Granny was always calling her clan to "come 'n' git" some of her delicious "vittles," usually some nauseating variation of possum stew or roast squirrel. "Vittles" sounds right for foods like that, but actually Granny was speaking more correctly than many theoretically more educated folk who, like us, thought *victual* was properly pronounced "vic-tu-al."

Just as Granny said, it's "VIT-l," whether you're talking about boiled possum or coquilles Saint-Jacques. *Victual* comes from the Anglo-French word *vitaylle* from the Old French word *vitaille*. You'll notice that in both cases there's no *c*. And that's how it has been pronounced in English since the times of William the Conqueror.

Long before William, however, there was a *c* in the word. The French got their word from the Romans and their Latin word *victualia* (provisions). When later Renaissance scholars in England realized this, they wanted the *c* back in to show how prestigious and classical English could be. But although they changed the spelling, the pronunciation didn't change—and *victual* was and is pronounced just like Granny said, in Oxford and her hometown of Bug Tussle alike.

viognier

[vee-ohn-YAY]

a white wine grape, originally grown in France's northern Rhone region, that produces a floral, fruity wine; also the wine produced from the grape

If you aren't familiar with this wine but know even a smattering of French, you probably can figure out how this is pronounced. But the decidedly un-English letter combinations flummox the rest of us: "Vyognee-er"? "Vioh-nyer"? "Vog-ner"? It is pronounced how it's spelled . . . in French, that is, with the *gn* sounding like *ni* (as in *bunion*) and the *ier*, a long *a*.

The word itself was first used in the mid-nineteenth century, but no one is quite sure about its origins. Some think it is a mash-up of Vienne (a Northern Rhone city where the grapes were grown) and Viagava (an island off the Dalmatian coast from which the vine was reportedly imported). But Vienne doesn't have the right sound, and Viagava hasn't been proven to be the source of the vine, so this theory doesn't hold water (or should that be wine?).

Before the 1980s, you'd have had to be quite the oenophile to know this wine. In the 1960s, it was only planted in about eight acres in France's Northern Rhone area. Now it's the most widely planted white Rhone varietal in the United States. You know it's no longer scarce when even Trader Joe's has its own viognier.

voile

[VOY-ull]

*a semitransparent fabric, often used
for curtains, blouses, and dresses*

With *voile*, we have yet another French import that has
been anglicized. So it technically isn't "vwahl" as the French
would say, but the oh-so-*not*-French "VOY-ull" (which
rhymes with *foil*).

It comes directly from the Old French *voil* or *voile*,
meaning "veil," which in turn comes from the Latin
velum. According to the *OED*, it first popped up in written
English in the late 1800s, and since then there have been
no variations on spelling or meaning. But pronunciation is
another matter entirely. Yes, it's "VOY-ull" in English, but
many fashionistas and fabric experts go with the French
"vwahl"—so you won't get into trouble if you pronounce it
either way. But should you run across the similarly spelled
fabric *toile*, well, just don't ask for "TOY-ull. It is "twahl."
After all, this is English where the rules often don't apply!

HOW TO SOUND LIKE A
SEASONED TRAVELER

The Correct Pronunciation for Seventeen of the
Most Commonly Mispronounced Place Names

Bangkok (Thailand): BHANG-gawk

Budapest (Hungary): boo-da-PESHT

Colombia: co-LOHM-bee-ya

Dominica: dom-i-NEEK-ah

Dubai: du-BYE

Iran: ee-RAHN

Iraq: ee-RAHK

Marseilles (France): mahr-SAY

Niger: nee-ZHAIR

Pakistan: PAK-uh-stan

Phuket (Thailand): poo-KE(t) (Thai is a tonal language,
and to be more correct, "poo" is spoken using a
normal voice tone; "ket" is a lower tone, with
the k a bit like a g, and a soft t at the end)

Qatar: kuh-tahr or gut-tahr

Quebec (Canada): kuh-BEK or kih-BEK (in Canada);
kwi-BEK (in the United States and the UK)

Tijuana (Mexico): tee-WHA-na

Vancouver (Canada): van-KOO-ver

Versailles (France): vers-EYE

Worcester (UK): WOO-ster

Wagner (Richard)

[VAH-gner]

nineteenth-century German composer known principally for his operas, such as the famous four-cycle "Ride of the Valkyries"

Richard Wagner was famous for his concept of *Gesamtkunstwerk* (total work of art), which combined poetic, visual, musical, and dramatic art into one as realized in his *Der Ring des Nibelungen*. And herein we already see a problem with Wagner for most English speakers—all that German!

It begins with his name, which is not pronounced as it looks to us but as "Ree-khard" (slightly gutteral-sounding *c*) "VAH-gner." The "Ree-khard" may sound pretentious to some, so stick with "Richard." As for *Wagner*, as long as you pronounce the *w* with a *v* sound and include a long *ah* sound afterward, you're doing fine. German does not have a *w* sound as we know it, hence all those jokey dialogues with Germans saying "You vill do it!" (Technically, Germans do have an unvoiced *w* sound, as in their word for wood, w*ald,* which sounds very different from the similar English *wood.* The English *w* sound requires much more rounding and tension in the lips; and so to us, when Germans say *w,* it sounds a lot more like a *v.*)

Incidentally, there's a Wagner College in New York named after the composer, but it's now pronounced as it looks: Wagner College. Whew!

wassail

[WOSS-uhl]

noun: spiced ale or mulled wine typically drunk at Christmastime; verb: to drink copiously and enjoy oneself in a loud, lively way; to go caroling during the Christmas season

The word *wassail* conjures up images of Christmas, Dickensian characters lustily singing Christmas carols, and cups of mulled wine, which is well and good . . . as long as you don't also think of sails. Because there is no "sail" in *wassail* in spite of appearances.

Wassail dates back to the late 1100s when it was a salutation in Old Norse consisting of *ves* (be) *heill* (healthy). But it wasn't connected with drinking at the time and was more of a "hail fellow, well met" greeting. It appears that the drinking aspect of *wassail* began when Danish speakers in England began using it as a toast, the equivalent of "bottoms up" or "prosit," and the phrase caught on with non-Danes as well. In fact, by the twelfth century, invading Normans thought of *wassail* as the epitome of Englishness. In time it was also used to mean the specific alcoholic beverage with which one used to toast (especially the spiced ale or mulled wine drunk during the Christmas holidays). Wassailing—when carolers go door to door at Christmas—was a fairly late addition, first being recorded in print in 1742.

Wednesday

[WENS-day]

*the day of the week following Tuesday
and preceding Thursday*

This is a tricky one because the right way to pronounce *Wednesday* is the way most people do: "WENS-day." Those people who think they're looking clever and being oh-so-proper by saying "WED-nez-day" are actually doing the opposite.

Wednesday is spelled the way it is because it evolved from the Old English *wodnesdaeg* (Woden's Day—*Woden* referring to the god Odin), which itself was the Germanic evolution from the Latin for Mercury's Day, *dies Mercurii*, since Odin was the Nordic Mercury. In spite of the spelling, even back in the fifteenth century people were pronouncing it with the contraction, as we still (properly) do. Interestingly, Germany, one of the traditional homes of Odin worship, de-Odinized their Wednesdays. Poor Odin was tossed by the wayside back in the tenth century, and Wednesday became *Mittwoch* (midweek) instead.

wintry

[WIN-tree]

characteristic of or pertaining to winter, cold

Even some weatherpeople pronounce this word with an extra syllable—as "WIN-ter-ee" instead of correctly as "WIN-tree." There are also numerous instances when *wintry* is written incorrectly as *wintery*. But *wintry* is the preferred and often the only form in dictionaries, so it's best to pronounce it with two, not three syllables: "WIN-tree."

If you want to quibble, both pronunciations and spellings can be justified. *Wintry* comes from the Old English *wintrig*—which in turn comes from the Old High German *wintirig*, which includes that extra syllable. But the *OED* sternly recognizes only two syllables and so should we (although the more accommodating *Merriam-Webster* now allows for "WIN-ter-ee"). If *wintry* was good enough for a cold English weather authors like Spencer, Shelley, Scott, Dryden, and Dickens, it's good enough for us.

would have

[wood hav]

indicating an action or state that didn't occur that was conditional upon another action or state that didn't occur in the past

"Would have" shouldn't be in a collection of shibboleths. It is a simple phrase consisting of two simple words, so how can anyone get it wrong? But many people do, by using an *of* in place of the *have*.

In fairness, in speech, the contraction *would've* sounds a lot like "would of," so we suspect some people are being maligned unfairly. We will give what might be a verbal "would of" a pass. But anyone who *writes* it "would of"—and doesn't later realize it was a phonetic transcription that should never have occurred—should turn in their smart person membership card.

Here is a basic rule of thumb you can share with people who are *of*-ing their way to shame: If you aren't sure whether to use *of* or *have* in a phrase, just take the verb (*could*, *would*, *should*, etc.) out of the sentence and see if it still works. "I could have danced all night" then becomes "I have danced all night," which makes a lot more sense than "I of danced all night" (which isn't even a sentence anymore). That should've—not should of—cleared things up.

xenophobia

[zen-uh-FOH-bee-uh]

intense dislike for people from foreign countries or foreign origins

Blame it on the ancient Greeks, who not only gave us the concept, but the word and their odd (to us) pronunciation. Yes, you probably know that the *x* is pronounced as a *z*, but many of us don't know that the preferred, educated pronunciation of the *e* is not with a long *e* sound but a short *e* (as in *Zen*).

The word *xenophobia* comes from two ancient Greek words—*xenos* (foreigner) and *phobia* (fear); and so it's clear from the word that hatred of foreigners stems from fear, not rationality. While we're on *xe* words derived from the ancient Greek, the inert atmospheric gas xenon is pronounced similarly, as "zennon," not "zeenon" as we pronounced it (incorrectly) in high school chemistry class.

Also note that *xeriscaping*, or dry-weather gardening (the coming thing in the dry western United States) is pronounced "zerr-eh-scaping," except in England, where it's "zeer-eh-scaping." But then again, in the wet British isles, they don't worry about the preferred pronunciation of what to them is probably a very foreign (*xenos*) concept.

yarmulke
(also yarmlke, yarmelke,
yarmolke, yarmulka)

[YAR-mull-kuh]

skullcap worn all the time by Orthodox Jewish men and for religious occasions by non-Orthodox Jewish men

Many people say "yamaka"—in a sort of "Japanese language meets Jewish culture" way. That's certainly what we heard all the time growing up in the New York area. In fact, we often wondered why it was spelled the way it was since it surely didn't sound the way it looked. It was a holdover from the past, we reasoned, wrongly.

As we've pointed out numerous times, just because many people say something doesn't mean it's right. And that's the case here. *Yarmulke* is actually correctly pronounced like it's spelled—with the *r* and the *l* firmly intact.

It was first noted in use in 1903 and evolved to its present spelling from the Yiddish *yarmolke,* which came, in turn, from the Polish *jarmulka* (cap). The latter was probably an offshoot of the Turkish word *yağmurluk* (rainwear) or maybe from the medieval Latin *almutia* (hood, cowl). Another theory is that it is derived from the Aramaic *yira malka* (awe of the King), but we were unable to find any substantiation of this from linguists. The point may be moot, though, as the Yiddish *yarmulke* is losing ground to the Hebrew word for dome, *kippah.*

yin-yang

[yin yang]

Chinese philosophical term emphasizing the interaction of complementary opposites—the yin or feminine principle (dark, wet, cold, passive) and the yang or masculine principle (bright, active)

"Crystal wore a ying-yang symbol as a pendant hanging from a chain around her neck, signifying that she lived in complete harmony with the world around her" (*Urban Dictionary*). No, Crystal wore a *yin*-yang symbol—no *g* in *yin*.

It's a common mistake. Most of us know that famous symbol that looks like a black and white six and nine joined, and many of us use the words, symbolizing the joining of complementary opposites. But a plethora of us say or write "ying-yang" (or "ying and yang" for *yin and yang*). Maybe because yin and yang are complementary opposites, it seems more correct to balance the *g* in *yang* with a *g* in *ying*. Whatever the reason, *ying-yang* versus *yin-yang* is quite prevalent. But as any Chinese philosopher could tell you, it's also quite wrong.

zoology

[zoh-OLL-uh-gee]

the study of animals

This appears quite straightforward—there's "zoo," the place where they keep animals, and "-ology," right? But look at it again. It isn't "zoo" at all. It is "zo" (from the Greek *zoion*, animal) that precedes the -ology (from the Greek *-logia*, study). For it to have the *oo* sound, it technically would need another *o* to form "zoo-ology."

But this is being a bit pedantic. In the UK, "zoo-OLL-uh-gee" is the common pronunciation, and a fair number of zoologists themselves pronounce it that way as well. If people in the field think it's "zoo," it's difficult to defend the ostensibly proper pronunciation. In fact, since so many people are more accustomed to saying it "ZOO-OLL-uh-gee," it is becoming, although not the preferred pronunciation, an accepted one. The *American Heritage Dictionary* panel reviewed the word and, in 1999, 60 percent of them determined that the "oo" pronunciation was acceptable. (In fact, while 68 percent said they used the proper "oh," 32 percent admitted to pronouncing it "oo.")

Side note: *Zoo* is actually short for zoological garden. So shouldn't we be calling a zoo a "zoh"?

zydeco

[ZAYH-duh-koh]

Louisiana Creole dance music combining blues, rhythm and blues, and traditional Creole music from the early Acadian settlers; usually features an accordion and a washboard

"Leh zayh-dee-co nuh sohn pah salay." This is roughly how someone speaking Louisiana Creole French would say the dance tune title "Les haricots sonts pas sales." Thus the word for the catchy dance music *zydeco* was born from how the title sounded.

Well, that's the more colorful version. Some say instead that the word came from a portmanteau of the Atakapan (an indigenous people who lived by the Gulf of Mexico) words for dance, *shi* (pronounced "shy"), and youths, *ishol*, which the visiting Spaniards changed to *zy ikol*; or that it evolved from a West African language. But since the venerable *Oxford English Dictionary* subscribes to the "Les haricots" theory and because it's a bit more fun, like the music itself, so will we.

It seems to fit best, since zydeco grew out of the music played at impromptu dances at people's homes. It was then typically just called French music or *le musique Creole*. In 1929, a group called the Zydeco Skillet Lickers recorded a song. This was possibly the first "official" use of the term, but over time, the term *zydeco* caught on and the music became more and more popular and widespread. So *laissez les bons temps rouler!*

ENDNOTES

aerie: "The pronunciation . . .adequately explained." *Oxford English Dictionary*. 2nd ed., s.v. "aerie."

chutzpah: "Rattle the . . . in loch." Leo Rosten, *The New Joys of Yiddish: Completely Updated* (New York: Harmony, 2003), 81.

Cthulhu: "The actual . . . being unrepresented." H. P. Lovecraft, *Selected Letters of H. P. Lovecraft V (1934–1937)* (Sauk City, Wisconsin: Arkham House, 1976), 10–11.

detritus: "Stuff left . . . word means." *Urban Dictionary*, s.v. "detritus," last modified June 2, 2005, http://www.urbandictionary.com/define.php?term=detritus.

diaeresis: "is in English an obsolescent symbol." H. W. Fowler, *A Dictionary of Modern English Usage* (New York & Oxford: Oxford University Press, 1965), 128.

Don Juan: "Till, after . . . Don Juan." Lord Byron, *Don Juan, Vol. 1* (London: John Murray, 1837), 53.

Dr. Seuss: "You're wrong . . . (or Zoice)." Donald E. Pease, *Theodor SEUSS Geisel* (Oxford: Oxford University Press, 2010), 54.

dull as ditch water: "digne . . . water." Pierce the Plowman's Crede (c. 1394), 375.

homage: "The people . . . a break!" Jeffrey A. Dvorkin, "The Joy of Text," NPR, November 23, 2004, http://www.npr.org/templates/story/story.php?storyId=4184266.

Houston: "As to . . . knowledge." William Pierce, "CXIX. William Pierce: Character Sketches of Delegates to the Federal Convention," in Max Farrand, The Records of the Federal Convention of 1787, Vol. 3, (New Haven, Conn.: Yale University Press, 1911), 97.

kibosh: "[P]ut the . . . her, Mary." Charles Dickens, *Sketches by Boz* (Philadelphia: Carey Lee & Blanchard, 1837), 85.

lackadaisical: "Goodlackaday! . . . thought it!" Henry Fielding, *Tom Jones, vol. II* (London: Sherwood, Neely, and Jones, 1818), 257.

machination: "Miss— . . . Normal School." "There can . . . rather ignorance." Henry Barnard, *The American Journal of Education* 17, 1867: 727.

mauve: "Only idiots . . . 'mauve' 'mawv." *Urban Dictionary*, s.v. "mauve," last modified November 6, 2004, http://www.urbandictionary.com/define.php?term=Mauve.

nip it in the bud: "Yet I . . . the bud." J. Fletcher, *Woman Hater* (London: Humphrey Moseley, 1648), Act III, Scene 1.

poinsettia: "Sixtyone million . . . took home." "The Poinsettia's Name Commonly Mispronounced," *Gwinnett Daily Post*, December 13, 2006, http://www.gwinnettdailypost.com/archive/thepoinsettiasnamecommonlymispronounced/article_9a7401ba309b5f81b8b23647e4da343b.html.

prestigious: "often an . . . use it." William Strunk and E. B. White, *The Elements of Style* (New York: Penguin, 2007), 85.

preventive: "Avoidance of . . . usage guides." *Oxford English Dictionary*, "preventative." Oxford University Press, 2016. http://www.oed.com.ezproxy.spl.org:2048/view/Entry/151075?redirectedFrom=preventative#eid.

prostrate: "Stop calling . . . with you?" "Prostrate vs. Prostate Cancer Difference Explained," *Happy Hospitalist*, http://thehappy hospitalist.blogspot.com/2012/07/ProstratevsProstateCancer ExplainedeCardHumor.html.

quinoa: "A kinde . . . do rice." Jan Huygen van Linschoten, Discours of voyages into ye Easte & West Indies, trans. William Phillip (London: John Windet for Iohn Wolfe printer to ye Honorable Cittie of London, 1598), 282.

schadenfreude: "Schadenfreude . . . not you." Natalie Venetia Belcon; Rick Lyon "Schadenfreude [Explicit]," *Avenue Q* (2003 Original Broadway Cast) (Masterworks Broadway, 2003, CD).

sherbet: "the costly Shurbets of Constaninople." George Sandys, *A Relation of a Journey Begun An: Dom: 1610: Fovre Bookes. Containing a Description of the Turkish Empire, of Ægypt, of the Holy Land, of the Remote Parts of Italy, and Ilands Adioyning* (London: W. Barrett, 1621) (second edition), 12.

sough: "The strange . . . pine tops." Isabella Lucy Bird, A Lady's Life in the Rocky Mountains (London: J. Murray, 1879), 101.

tenet: "Irving Yalom . . . human existence." Bonnie Smith Crusells, "Death Anxiety," in *Encyclopedia of Psychology and Religion*, ed. David A. Leeming Ph.D. et al. (New York: Springer Publishing, 2010), 211–12.

theater: "characteristic chiefly of uneducated speech."
Dictionary.com. *Dictionary.com Unabridged*. Random House,
Inc. http://www.dictionary.com/browse/theater.

Tolkien (J. R. R.): "I am . . . as keen." J. R. R. Tolkien, *The Letters of
J. R. R. Tolkien* (Boston: Houghton Mifflin, 2014), 428.

Uranus: "Can I . . . too, Lavender?" J. K. Rowling, *Harry Potter and
the Goblet of Fire* (New York: Scholastic, 2000), 201.

vehicle: "in Standard . . . never pronounced." H. W. Fowler,
Fowler's Dictionary of Modern English Usage (New York & Oxford:
Oxford University Press, 2015), 857.

ABOUT THE AUTHORS

Ross Petras and Kathryn Petras are a brother-and-sister writing and editing team, with over 5.2 million copies of their work in print—including titles such as *Very Bad Poetry*, *Wretched Writing*, *Age Doesn't Matter Unless It's a Cheese,* and the annual calendar *The 365 Stupidest Things Ever Said.* Their work has been featured in the *New York Times, Chicago Tribune, Wall Street Journal, Playboy, Cosmopolitan, Washington Post, Huffington Post*, and the *London Times.* They have appeared on hundreds of radio and TV shows including *Good Morning America*, CNN, and *Fox and Friends.* Ross collects (and sells) rare books (chiefly early printed books in Latin and Greek). He reads, writes, or speaks, with (very varying) degrees of proficiency, Latin, Greek, Arabic, and French, and loves reading—and watching—vintage sci-fi and 1930s romantic comedy. Kathy is a noir film and pulp novel fiend, a bad joke aficionado, does computer-generated graphic art, and is proud to say she was on *Jeopardy!* (but, sadly, came in third—and won only a designer watch). Both of them are word nuts, quote connoisseurs, and (they must admit) sometimes annoying grammar pedants. Ross lives in Toronto, Kathy in Seattle.

Library of Congress Cataloging-in-Publication Data
Names: Petras, Ross, author. | Petras, Kathryn, author.
Title: You're saying it wrong : a pronunciation guide to the 150 most
  commonly mispronounced words—and their tangled histories of
  misuse / Ross Petras, Kathryn Petras.
Description: Berkeley : Ten Speed Press, 2016. | Includes
  bibliographical references and index.
Subjects: LCSH: English language—Pronunciation. | English language—
  Pronunciation—History. | English language—Pronunciation—Social
  aspects. | English language—Errors of usage. | English language—
  Errors of usage—Social aspects. | English language—Usage—History.
  | English language—Usage—Social aspects. | BISAC: LANGUAGE
  ARTS & DISCIPLINES / Linguistics / General. | SOCIAL SCIENCE /
  Popular Culture. | LANGUAGE ARTS & DISCIPLINES / Vocabulary.
Classification: LCC PE1137 .P448 2016 (print) | LCC PE1137 (ebook) |
  DDC 421/.54—dc23
LC record available at https://lccn.loc.gov/2016015511

Hardcover ISBN: 978-0-399-57808-3
eBook ISBN: 978-0-399-57809-0

Printed in the United States of America

Design by Chloe Rawlins

10 9 8 7 6 5 4 3 2 1

First Edition